Shades of Suicide

Open verdict/suicide bereavement

Ann M Davies

Publisher March Hare UK

ISBN: 0-9552506-0-9
978-0-9552506-0-6

Edited by Professor John Goodridge
Nottingham Trent University

Printed by www.catfordprint.co.uk

Publisher
March Hare UK
22 Tollerton Park, Tollerton, Nottingham, NG12 4 GD, UK
Tel: 0781 55 09 33

Front cover: Izu Peninsula Japan

Part One
The Event

Preface

On Tuesday 1st July 2003 a press release issued by the Royal College of Psychiatrists came into the public domain, it was entitled 'New Study reveals aspects of suicide bereavement never identified before.' The study examined the reactions and experiences of parents who had lost their children, between the ages of 16 and 35, as a result of suicide. The synopsis posted on the Internet highlighted the lack of attention given to the needs of parents bereaved in this manner. It also drew attention to the fact that, for every person who dies by their own hand, at least seven to ten people are profoundly affected by the event.[1]

Joint statistics for 'Suicide and Undetermined Deaths' (produced by the Samaritans for 2002) recorded a total of 5882 deaths in that year.[2] If between seven to ten people are profoundly affected by such an event, it can be estimated that between 30,000 to 50,000 people in the United Kingdom will experience varying degrees of distress by the loss of someone very close or important to them as a result of suicide, open verdict, undetermined death and other terms used, when the circumstances of the death do not allow an unequivocal statement of death by suicide.

In September 2003 I was traumatically bereaved by the loss of a friend, business partner and close companion of 22 years. The Coroner declared at the inquest an outcome of 'Open Verdict'. I was fortunate to have a support network of friends and family around me who protected, strengthened and guided me through this uncharted territory, but at times I longed to be with someone who had walked this particular road ahead of me. I searched for this companionship within the few books I found about suicide bereavement, where individuals related their experiences, albeit only briefly. A year after my bereavement, however, I came across Robert Dykstra's book – *She Never Said Goodbye*[3] - written in the 1980's which is a much fuller personal account of suicide bereavement and I found this a great comfort. Even though his circumstances were different, I recognised a very similar grief, anguish and questioning.

Many years previous to my own loss, I had been involved in presenting some weekend retreats for the bereaved. I recalled how difficult it had been at that time to find anything written for people bereaved by suicide, in all its many shades, but I had come across one book entitled *The Special Scar*[4]. The first edition of this book was printed in 1991. I had located this book in the early nineties, by dint of scouring bookshops. I came across it in one of those 'off beat - off the high street' shops. Years later - but only eighteen months prior to Tonie's death - I passed this book on to someone bereaved by suicide saying, "I will not need this and it may help you." How little we know of what lies ahead of us!

After Tonie's death I began searching the bookshops once again for literature dealing with loss through suicide. Once again the book *A Special Scar* now in a second edition, and in a mainstream bookshop, came to hand. Trawling the Internet I found reference to innumerable books, extracts from journals and articles relating to the subject of suicide itself, yet only limited writing from the viewpoint of those bereaved through suicide. Most of the personal accounts of suicide bereavement are brief, a few pages at most, and contained within books of a more general nature, such as self-help books for bereavement through suicide. Yet I was thankful for these brief insights into how others had experienced their bereavement, even though the actual circumstances were totally different from my own. It felt like belonging to an 'unknown family' and gave me a sense of anchorage. At times when I was on my own, and felt that my experience of loss was overwhelming me, I would pick up the books and read these snippets. I found this brought calmness and comfort. Nevertheless, at the beginning of my journey, I still longed for a personal account of more depth and detail. It is the lack of literature giving a detailed account of one person's bereavement by suicide, that has led me to write about my particular circumstances.

In order to contextualise my bereavement I need to relate a little about myself and the background to the tragic events, which tore my life apart.

I was born June 8th 1947 and brought up in Catholic Lancashire. From as far back as I can recall I have always had a sense of the presence of God, nurtured and fired within the Catholic environment into which birth thrust me. According to my mother I am reported to have said at the age of five, "I am going to be one of those ladies in black," referring to the nuns who were employed as head teachers in the local authority Roman Catholic schools I attended. I have no recollection of this declaration. Nevertheless, I do remember vividly the day when, at the age of seven, I received the Eucharist. The sense of the presence of God was so powerful that to this day the memory of that first reception of the Eucharist has left its indelible trace.

From the age of seven or eight, I would on weekdays, before school, get up early and walk alone to Mass, a distance of about a mile, return home for my breakfast and then walk back again to school, which lay in the shadow of the church. The attraction to the presence of Christ in the Eucharist and that spirituality of worship and prayer has permeated my whole life for the past fifty years. Therefore, my experience of, and response to Tonie's death is coloured by my unbroken relationship with God embodied in thirty-five years of consecrated life and Roman Catholic spirituality.

After the vagaries of youth and early adulthood, I found myself continually drawn towards religious life within the Roman Catholic Church. I spent ten years in a semi-contemplative religious community, departing in 1980 to pursue a consecrated life outside the established institutional norm of that time. Those ten years nurtured within me an ever deepening love for Christ; a love of prayer and silence; a love of service and engagement with people and with life itself.

In 1981 Tonie joined me and we began a life together built on a commitment to prayer, to apostolic work and to each other. We spent twenty-two years together living a consecrated life of community, prayer and service. For those who are not familiar with the concept of consecrated life, it means, broadly, committing your life to God through prayer and worship, as well as giving love and care to those whose lives you share, but excludes sexual relationships. An awareness and love for God that draws you to prayer, worship, and a love and care for others animate this lifestyle. This has the characteristic of being all-inclusive rather than the more exclusive love that is implied in a couple to couple or family relationship.

Tonie had never been particularly robust in health; her childhood had been one of separation and alienation from her birth family, followed by traumatic experiences in her long term foster home. She had attempted suicide once before - twenty-five years earlier - followed by a year in hospital, receiving treatment and counselling in preparation for rehabilitation back into normal day-to-day life.

Two years later in August 1981 we embarked on our shared consecrated life. Tonie was physically and mentally well and we were both full of enthusiasm and hope for our future. A period of eighteen stable and happy years ensued. Then, in 2001, Tonie was diagnosed with Chronic Fatigue Syndrome or M.E. This was preceded by two years of intermittent periods when she had felt generally unwell, but no cause could be found for her problems.

Looking back, perhaps this was the beginning of the downward spiral into a dramatic and deep depression, which in September 2003 took her from me and all those who loved and cared for her. By this time she had also entered the menopausal period of her life. I believe that all of these factors, along with what I think must have been an unfathomable and uncontrollable urge within her towards self-destruction, led to her tragic and totally unexpected death.

At the inquest the Coroner pronounced 'open verdict' from the evidence collected relating to Tonie's death. Nevertheless, even though the circumstances of her death could not be determined as a clear-cut verdict of suicide, in my heart I know that there was a moment in time, when life seemed totally unbearable to her. She had left our home with the intention of ending her life. Her thoughts and feelings in those final hours can only be speculative for us who are left behind. The fact that she had taken a fillet knife, along with a large dose of co-proxomal would seem to indicate her intentions. However, the knife was never used, and even the quantity of co-proxomal taken could not be stated as the sole cause of death, hence, the Coroner's conclusion of an 'open verdict'.

The recollections and reflections, which follow, are not about Tonie's life. I believe that it is not my place to recount her story. Tonie was an extremely private person and to divulge her experiences would be, for me, a betrayal of her trust and our friendship. This book is about my life since losing her to what appears as a self-chosen death. Yet it is my belief, that many suicides, though of course not all, are not self-chosen deaths but caused by an irrepressible urge towards self-destruction, which in the final analysis can no longer be contained. I have come to this belief from the accounts given to me from some of those who have survived suicide. They explain that their emotional pain was so unbearable that an inner force welled up in them, far greater than the instinct for survival, which drove them to attempt self-annihilation.

The title of the book Shades of Suicide is not accidental. It embodies the truth that suicide has thousands of shades, it crosses every culture, age, situation, occupation, religious or non-religious style of living. The circumstances are unique to each individual and the means to death are varied. Because of this diversity it is likely that some of you will not identify with the views or reflections expressed within my account. Yet, by contrasting your views and thoughts with mine, you may be able to clarify your experience of bereavement through suicide. In that process of seeking, I hope you will find some answers to your unique passage through shock, grief and loss and feel less alone as you tread this tortuous path. Another reason for the title, 'Shades of Suicide', is that the event takes you into the 'Shades', a place of obscurity, a place where you feel screened off from the rest of the world, a place where shade and darkness predominate. Even so, as often happens in shady places, gentle shafts of light permeate here and there to help you find your way ahead. These gentle shafts of light are the kind words, understanding and love we receive from others.

The Coroner delivered a conclusion of 'open verdict' in relation to Tonie's death, but for ease of reading I will use the term 'suicide' to refer to all deaths that lie in the shade of the term suicide; terms such as open verdict, undetermined cause. There is however, no implication that by using the term 'suicide' for all these shades, I am suggesting that the person you have lost, consciously and deliberately took their own life. The use of the word 'suicide' throughout is a literary decision made for ease of reading, and allows me to encompass those verdicts, which lie within its shade.

Every single day there are people whose lives, like ours, are ravaged by suicide. We are in this tragedy together. Perhaps, by reading this book, you will experience that while you are on your own, because each death of this nature is individual, you are never entirely alone. Others, from far and wide, ride the waves of grief with you day by day. In addition, there are people, who through prayer, commend your grief to the healing power of the spirit of God; others of no particular religious persuasion, or who have no belief in a life beyond death, give their time to listen and to care about your grief - my grief in the present. Scientists, medics, researchers and others work towards trying to find answers to this continuing phenomenon in the life and existence of humanity. If we bring each of these strands to mind, they can give us hope and strength when we feel the future is bleak and our grief is overwhelming us.

It is beyond words for us to convey to others the full reality of the emotional shock and disbelief that death through a suicide brings. This book is an attempt to impart something of that experience, to weave another strand into the care that exists around us, to help us to deal with our grief. It is to walk in the shades with you the reader, whether you are the bereaved closest to the person you have lost to suicide, a relative, a friend, or someone who has, in some way, been affected by suicide and you are searching to come to terms with this life changing event.

May a shaft of light permeate the shades in which you walk.

* All the names apart from my own have been altered to preserve the privacy of those who were caught up with me in this tragic event.

September 19th 2004

Darkness has fallen. I park the car well off the unlit road and look around for the torch I had intended to bring. I have left it behind. What does it matter - I know the way only too well.

Stepping out of the car I throw my anorak hood over my head; the night is set, a brisk breeze and a slight drizzle are my companions. Tonight I have dressed in dark clothing so that I blend into the night. There are no stars in the sky, only clouds scudding above the earth, blotting out any light that may have radiated from the stars. A couple of cars speed past, through the seamless darkness, water swishing over their wheels, their lights penetrating the night as their drivers travel to their destinations. I am thankful for the anonymity of the dark, dismal night and the lack of interest in my movements from those who pass by.

Going through the swing gate I make out the path; it is a shade lighter than its surroundings. I focus on the light-coloured ground to get my bearings, then start walking.

On my own in the late hours I feel no fear or threat as I trudge along. Stones crunch beneath my feet and pools of water plop as I step into them. I look around me and in the distance notice lights being switched on in bedrooms, they are like full stops punctuating the darkness - people off to bed. Gradually, my eyes adjust and I discern the outline of the hedge defining my path.

I am still not quite sure why I am here. Is it to re-affirm the fact of her death? Is it to try and understand a little more of something that I will never understand? I walk on.

The anguish of her loss, the trauma of her leaving, the sadness of the circumstances of her death has wrought a change in me. I would never have dreamt of walking on my own late at night, as I am now, down an unlit, lonely country pathway. My awareness of the transitory nature of earthly life is more acute than ever. I am not concerned about my own death, be it today, tomorrow, next week, next year. Only the present moment matters because that is all there is. As each moment ticks by, the past, a slippery fish eludes the grasp, never to be caught, it slides away. The present moves on, taking me towards an anticipated future, but also one that might never be.

My mind flits briefly to the first time I trod this path. I do not stay with the memory. I am concerned with this moment in time, with my urge to come here tonight, not really sure why.

Looking ahead I search the night for the shrub on the left of the path. That is where the pool is. Opposite the pool is the hedge. Behind the hedge is the ditch. The ditch was her grave. It was here that she died and decomposed to such a degree that when she was found the person who discovered her said "I thought it was a body, but I was not sure!" I walk on - then stop. Yes, I think this is the spot. I bend down and feel with my hands for the fuchsia Kieran and I had planted some weeks ago alongside the path and by the hedge. My hand comes upon it almost immediately. I sit down on the grass verge trying to push myself as far under the hedge as I can to shelter from the rain. I can see little and the only sound reaching my ears is the rustling of leaves. I am right by the ditch where she laid waiting for death. I sit alone. I still don't quite know why I feel so compelled to be here. I decide to curl up beneath the hedge as near as I can to the ditch on the other side of the hedge, as near to the place she died as I can be. I didn't have the chance to be with her as she lay dying; I couldn't assure her of my love and care; we couldn't talk to one another about the separation her death would bring. Perhaps that is why I am lying here under the hedge on this September night just one year since she died, trying to be close to her.

A deep sense of peace comes to me. The earth gives off its warmth and the comforting smell of the damp soil soothes and strengthens. I lie here not really thinking about anything - just being - when the words come to me - *Ann why are you looking for me here, I am not here in this ditch, I am with you wherever you are, as much as I ever was. Instead of lying here go and give comfort and hope to others who have been bereaved by suicide. Help people to understand us, to love us, not to condemn us, to talk about us, not to be ashamed of us.*

I don't hear her voice, and yet, I am conscious that the words are not my thoughts, that they exist not outside my mind, but outside my conscious thought processes. It might be accurate to say I hear her in my 'mind's ear'. I stay where I am.

This is not what I expected, I had anticipated crying, an attempt on my part to re-live that terrible night, to somehow 'get inside her skin', to understand. Instead, here I am experiencing peace, a sense that all is well. The words of the mystic and anchoress of the fourteenth century - Julian of Norwich - come to mind: 'All shall be well and all manner of things shall be well'. A cognisance of the shortness of life etches out in sharp relief in my consciousness. Almost two thirds of an average lifespan has passed, so while I grieve for Tonie I believe I must also live creatively with what time I have left. I lay a while longer curled up under the hedge, then my mind turns to the rubber glove. I know I am nearer to it than I have been before; it is within my reach.

A piece of rubber; the casual passer-by might notice it, attached to a branch, quivering in the wind. It could be a deflated balloon, or perhaps a discarded condom blown from its point of usefulness and caught here in the hedge. But no, it is just the remnants of a rubber glove, which has become charged with significance, because it is the glove used to mark the place of her death. A member of the forensic team hung it there after they had recovered her body. As I lie in the darkness, I ponder on how the glove has been a beacon through the dark, devilish days of shock. It has been an anchor in the storm raging around me, a rock on which to hold tenaciously. This is a strange contradiction, a flimsy rubber glove has felt like a rock onto which my mind has clung and my spirit derived strength. I had resolved that one day I must remove it. Now is the time, I am ready to take another step forward into the future.

I push myself further forward under the hedge and peer into the shades of the night. I see nothing, only darkness, but I know the glove is there. Wriggling forward on my stomach a little more, I stretch out to where I think the glove might be. I am right beneath the hedge now, the ditch is in front of me, and I grope to keep my balance, trying to prevent myself getting caught on the branches. Reaching upwards I pull down a strong twig towards me, there it is, I feel it, the rubber glove is in my hand. The twig is trying to spring away from me; it does not want to yield. I cling on firmly, then bending it with as much force as I can muster I snap off the end. Clasping the glove I experience a sense of relief. Gingerly, I back out from beneath the hedge. I can feel branches catching the back of my jacket and the muddy earth against my legs; slowly I re-emerge onto my side of the hedge.

Once more, resuming my place of shelter, I look across the field to the spots of illumination just a few hundred yards away that mark habitation. The path lies at my feet, people walked along here day after day during the time Tonie was missing, literally five feet away from where she lay dying and decaying. What irony, people so near and yet so far away!

As I had come to expect, during the time of waiting, it was dogs that found her. They arrived at the end of the food chain, which had fed on her body until the time of its discovery. I recall the words spoken in the Roman Catholic Liturgy each Ash Wednesday as the worshippers commence their Lenten observance. The priest anoints the person's forehead marking it with ashes formed from the burnt palms of the previous year and says to the recipient , 'Remember man that you are dust and unto dust you shall return.'

I look down at the glove in my hand. Did this glove actually touch her decomposed body? Was it worn by one of the forensic team? Was it a spare glove? These thoughts run through my mind. I decide it doesn't really matter, its purpose has been served.

I sit a while longer. The rain has lightened but the darkness remains. Yet, in that darkness, I experience peace, a sense of Tonie's goodness and wholeness – a strange paradox – peace and wholeness on this dark, dreary night. More thoughts skim across the surface of my mind. I recall some friends commenting that they believed Tonie had passed almost 'naturally' from this life to a life beyond. That she walked to a place where she was at one with the earth and nature, which she loved, and in that place the Eternal One had freed her from her mental and physical torment.

But, my anguish is still raw, sadness lingers and clings to the ever-changing memories, thoughts and feelings that batter my mind and body. The nearest description I can find to try and explain the ferocity of that internal battering is to liken the experience to that of storms and flooding. When violent storms and floods occur, one moment your home, your life and the people you love are safe and on solid ground. Then comes the floodwater and all that security is swept away with a force and violence beyond your control. The water rises, it covers the landmarks you know, the solid ground goes from under you, and so it is with the shock and grief of suicide. The experience batters and swamps your inner self, all that you know is destroyed, and grief is your constant companion. The experience is so violent that at times you desire that you will be consumed by death as a release from the anguish and pain of such a great loss.

The longing and wishing that I had understood Tonie's suffering, stings sharply and draws tears; the desire that her death had not come this way, the flood of doubt and guilt fluctuate as unyielding tides. Yet interweaving between these thoughts and emotions is the finest thread of spun steel. It bends and moves, it supports and carries but does not break. It is prayer in pain. It is stillness and silence in sadness. It is enduring love in loss.

Scrambling to my feet I walk purposefully towards the car. The night remains steeped in darkness, yet, in my heart and mind there is a glimmer of light, a perception, an unfathomable knowing that was not there when I walked into this field, into this night. The recent past now gone forever, held only in the mind, the future in the making ever becoming and awaiting.

September 19th 2003

Marking the end of my working day, I ensure the door is locked, put my briefcase into the back of the car, leave the building and head towards home. Glancing at my watch I note it is only 8.40. I will be home for 8.50. I have got away early as I promised.

That same morning I had cancelled Tonie's tuition commitments; she was feeling particularly ill with her Chronic Fatigue Syndrome. This strange and mystifying illness manifests itself in many ways. Dr. Anne Macintyre in her book *M.E. Chronic Fatigue Syndrome*[5] describes it as 'a potentially chronic and disabling disorder of the brain and muscles, and causes profound exhaustion, pain and mental confusion.' One of the contradictions of this illness is that one day the sufferer can hardly think or move, then the following day the symptoms will have receded as though they never existed.

During my short journey home, I wonder if Tonie will be well enough to go out the following day; Saturday. Often a Saturday afternoon affords us the opportunity to relax, to enjoy one another's company. We don't have to talk a great deal, there is a bond between us of quiet contentment, common goals and similar interests; we are soul mates.

Approaching the house, I look to see if the light in the lounge is on. No. She must still be feeling quite ill and has stayed in bed. I open the gate, park the car and head for the back door. No light on in her room. I unlock the door and call, as we always do to each other.

"Hi, where are you?"

Going to her bedroom, I see she isn't there. She must be lying on the settee. No, not there either. A little perplexed but not yet worried I think to myself. She must have gone down to a neighbour a few doors away, to have a chat. She has got bored with being on her own. I go back to her bedroom and put on the light to check that her nightclothes are on the bed, a sign that she has got dressed and gone out. Then I see the note. I read it. Shock tremors run through me. I know immediately that something dreadful has happened between leaving home at 12.45 and my return tonight. I walk slowly from her room into the kitchen and make myself a cup of coffee, trying to gather my thoughts.

With a cup of coffee in my hand, I walk around trying to think logically. Have the painkillers gone? What clothes has she put on? Yes, the tablets are missing. Clothes? I am not sure about this, as I am not very observant in this regard. Looking at the shoe rack I see her trainers and slippers have gone. From the coat rack her new green fleece and another coat are missing; this gives me some idea of what she might be wearing.

Looking at the clock, I see an hour has passed and it is almost ten. I had better ring someone to help me search for her. I stand in the kitchen thinking there is no one I can ring. This absurd thought is the first manifestation of my state of shock. There are many people I can ring who would be willing to go with me to look for her. But, at this moment, my mind is blank. Don't be ridiculous; think. I write down six names and telephone numbers. I ring one after the other, but there is no reply from anyone until the last call. "Nathan, something terrible has happened, Tonie has gone missing."

We talk, then decide that since he has had a drink with a meal only an hour earlier I will drive over to his home seven miles away and pick him up. We will return to my place then go out to look for her.

Approaching a roundabout on my way to meet Nathan I wonder whether I should first go into the local town centre and look for her there, before dragging Nathan out – perhaps she is just wandering around hoping that someone will see her. Round and round the island I drive, three or four times, in a state of indecision. This will not do, I say to myself. If I am to come through this trauma I must be decisive. I drive on.

It is the missing trainers that tell me she is unlikely to be walking the streets, that she is more likely to be somewhere in the countryside. She never wears trainers unless we are going for a walk on uneven ground. Her most likely route I think is along the canal towpath, but this is by no means a certainty, however, that is where we start our search.

By the time I collect Nathan and we are back at my place it is about 11.30 pm. Putting on suitable footwear and jackets, we collect torches and set off down the canal towpath.

Torchlight skims the surface of the canal. Nathan sweeps the beam over the water. I feel sick. "I don't think she would put herself in the canal, she hates water." I look along the edge of the path next to the hedge expecting to see her curled up at the side of the canal somewhere. It is only months later I note the irony of the situation and realise how accurate I was. The places we are looking for her now, in the first hour or two of this night, are similar to the place where she will eventually be found.

Tiredness and painful muscles are just two of the many symptoms of Chronic Fatigue Syndrome, so when we reach a crossroads where she could have veered from the towpath I say to Nathan, "I don't think she could have walked much further than this, she said she was in so much pain this morning. Her most likely route will have been to the right here, because by going left she would have come to houses." We turn into a wide track, used by farm vehicles to access the fields around and beyond.

Time has assumed a different perspective and meaning. As midnight passes Friday 19th September 2003 has slipped away. Now, it is Saturday September 20th and time is moving on, every moment taking me one step further away from Tonie and another step into an unknown future, but I want to go back, to replay those hours and to change the scene. I want my life to be 'normal' and not in the deep shades of this unexpected trauma.

Continuing our search, we look along hedgerows, under bushes, behind buildings. The night is relatively light and warm, maybe warmer than average for this time of the year. I am thankful for this because it may mean that she is safer than she would be if tonight were cold, wet and windy. No, I say to myself, it is not just the elements that are the danger; it is also the state of her mind and body that are threatening her survival.

Futile - this is the conclusion we reach after searching for about two hours; she could be anywhere. We walk back towards the car and discuss our next course of action. "Do you think I should ring the police?" I question. "Will they be interested - an adult missing and gone only for 12 hours, at the most?" We decide that I will ring the police, as Tonie might have been seen by someone, been taken to hospital and the police notified. First I collect an overnight bag so I can stay at Nathan's.

Half an hour later Nathan dials the number for the police and hands me the phone. Briefly, I explain the situation, and the police officer informs me that since Tonie has left a note they will deal with the problem immediately. However, I have to be back at our home at the point of the 'scene' and the police officers will meet me there. I arrange to meet them around 2.00 am. I tell Nathan I will return to the house alone, there is nothing he can do, and he needs to get some rest.

Standing outside our home, I gaze across the city into the night. Dazed, I wait for the police to arrive. I reflect on how calm and pleasant the night is, and find some small comfort in that. Two officers meet me and we go into the house. They note down brief details, read her note, take a look around the house and the area immediately adjacent to it, without finding anything of further significance. Assuring me that if Tonie is not home by the morning, a thorough search will be undertaken, they take their leave.

Sitting at the computer in these early hours of the morning, I type a letter ready to send out to our clients, to tell them about the situation and cancel all lessons forthwith. Then I recall Nathan's advice - keep eating even if you don't feel like it, and take some brandy before going to bed, it will help you cope with the shock. I take heed of that advice and go to bed.

By now it is around 3.30 am. I switch on the radio and the words of a familiar song come over loud and clear:

'We'll meet again don't know where, don't know when, but I know we'll meet again some sunny day, keep smiling through just like you always do till the blue skies drive the dark clouds far away ....'

It is a rendering of the song from a Johnny Cash album and is being played as part of a tribute to him. He had died on 12th September just a week ago today, and the songs of this particular album are focused on the theme of approaching death and his Christian belief.

No words could have been more appropriate to my situation. My mind blank and my body exhausted with shock I fall into a dreamless sleep.

September 20th 2003

My life has suddenly and unexpectedly been blown apart. I am spinning into an emotional 'black hole' where no boundaries can be perceived, there are no stars to light or guide, just nothingness.

It is the morning of Saturday September 20th 2003. I find a little notebook and write in the day and the date. I tell myself, I must try and keep track of the dates and the days and make some notes or else I will have no idea of time or of the order of events. Onward I go, spinning into my personal black hole, into a world of emotional anguish that no words can ever touch, moving through rather than being present to the world and the events around me; yet never alone because of the care and concern from family and friends.

In the midst of this nothingness there is also an awareness of being 'carried' on 'wings of prayer.' In the Old Testament the image of being carried 'on eagle's wings' is used to express the belief that God is with those whose burden is heavy. I feel as though I am being carried through this nightmare on 'eagle's wings.' That I am clinging onto the eagle as it transports me to great heights, through the darkness of this experience. I have no clue as to where I am being carried I just hang on. There are two sides to my experience of this trauma, the emotional nothingness of the black hole and the sense of a supporting presence in the image of the eagle. Oddly, while one part of my life is spinning out of control another part of me is focused with an amazing clarity.

A sense of urgency triggers me to send out letters to parents notifying them that there will be no tuition until further notice. I am already considering closing our business. Tonie and I offer specialist tuition to children with literacy difficulties. My intuition, arising from these events, that are swamping me, is that Tonie will not be found alive, and that if she is alive she will not be fit to teach, she will need my care. I cannot envisage continuing to run the business whatever the outcome.

As the day progresses people come and go. Our close friends Ian and Jean arrive. I see the shock and disbelief on their faces, as they and others go off to search for Tonie in the locality. The police organise a helicopter carrying a heat sensor to scour a two-mile radius around our home in a bid to detect her. As I sit out on the patio of our home, I look up at the helicopter moving slowly and methodically through the air. At this point I feel angry about all the fuss her disappearance is making, and think to myself, they will not find her it is just a waste of time. Having taken this step she will have no desire to try and climb out of the chasm in which she has found herself. The effort to get out will be too great; she must want to die. I think of how private a person Tonie is and know that if she is to be found alive she will be mortified by all the fuss her actions have caused. As awful as the thought is, I think it is better for her to die if that is what she wants.

During the afternoon the police search her room, and the immediate neighbourhood. They interview the neighbours and return with the news that the son of a neighbour had seen Tonie yesterday at around two o'clock in the afternoon. Also, around the same time, two women getting off a bus on the lane had seen her near to the turning into our road. Vince knows Tonie and he explains to the police how he had seen her walking along the lane carrying a plastic carrier bag, out of which hung a sharp knife. He had stopped his car, wound down his window and called to her, saying, "Tonie, do you know you have a sharp knife hanging out of your bag?" He told the police, and later me, that when she turned to look at him he was deeply shocked by her face. He said that her face was 'broken'. " She had a beautiful face didn't she?" He questioned. "But, her face looked so awful I could not make up my mind if it was her or not. I was so shocked by her face I did not even take note of what she was wearing, I was just transfixed by her face, I kept thinking to myself is it Tonie or not? I will remember her face forever. I asked her if she was okay, or if she needed any help. She didn't reply, there were tears in her eyes and she just turned and walked away. I was going to the chemist for my parents, I was only there about twenty minutes and so I thought I would look out for Tonie on my return journey but she was nowhere to be seen."

On hearing this news I look at the knives in the kitchen and sure enough, a brand new fillet knife, which Tonie had bought only a few weeks previously, is gone. Another shock. It never occurred to me that she might take a knife. I cannot imagine, and do not want to imagine, that she will harm herself in this way. I think back to the purchase of the knife. We had gone into a specialist kitchen shop, as we often did, just to look round. Tonie said that we needed a fillet knife. I was a little perplexed at the time of the purchase, as we have several very sharp knives. Yet Tonie was not one to waste money, or to say we needed something if we didn't, so she bought it and I thought nothing further of it. Now, I begin to ruminate on this. Was she thinking about suicide when she purchased the knife? The fact that she has taken the knife just adds to my conviction that she really has left with no intention of returning.

Later in the day I go to evening mass. Just before the service I am in the house near the church. The local news is on, and one of the news items is an appeal for any sightings of a man who had gone missing some days previously. I look across the room at Nathan and comment, "I suppose Tonie also may not be found for some time either, or even at all, this possibility had already crossed my mind." He nods in agreement. I glance down at a newspaper lying on the table and notice there is an article in the paper discussing suicide. The next moment, a preview appears on the television alerting viewers to a programme later in the week that will be looking back at the death of Marilyn Monroe. Only 48 hours into my own trauma I realise, yet again, I am not alone in this life-shattering event, people disappear, and people end their lives every day. What has changed is that I am no longer outside these events, I have joined an army of people who are left behind to face and deal with the consequences of such circumstances.

I make my way into the church and an elderly lady greets me, she asks me to read a prayer during the service. The person neither knows me nor is aware of my circumstances because this church is not my usual place of worship. Of all the prayers I might be asked to read out, the one I am given is a prayer for all those who have died recently. I do not know how I read out the prayer, somehow I do, I pray it for Tonie, I know she is dead.

I drive back home to meet my sister and brother-in-law. They have travelled up from the South to be with me. We sit and talk for ages, my brother-in-law keeps saying, "What's wrong with her, what more does she want? You've got a lovely home and a good business, no money worries, many friends, I can't understand it, it's crazy, it's crazy." I agree, but I know that is exactly what self-destruction is in the eyes of those whose minds are rational – crazy.

Later that night I lie in bed praying over and over again these words for Tonie, "Go in peace my friend." I cannot bear to think of her suffering so much, and know my only way to peace of mind is to begin the process of letting her go. This prayer is the first step of many more in a constant effort to come to terms with this tragic event and move on.

September 21st 2003

9.00 a.m. Sunday 21st September, and there is still no sign of Tonie. It is now 36 hours since I read her note. The police searched Tonie's room yesterday and found further scribblings revealing her distressed state of mind and her turmoil. Today they take hair samples from her hairbrush. I perceive this as the first sign, although they have not mooted the idea, that she may not be found alive. The police explain to me that the first routines in searching for Tonie have been completed, that there is a search procedure in place which they have to follow. It is now time for me to agree to a public appeal to go out on radio, teletext, and television for sightings of her. The telephone seems to be ringing continually and my sister deals with the calls, I find it impossible to talk to anyone over the phone.

Uppermost in my mind is to try and keep some hold on reality and, in my conviction that Tonie will be found dead I know that I must take steps to close down our business. I begin to direct all my energies into organising this. Otherwise the day passes as something of a daze. Late afternoon my brother-in-law leaves for home but my sister remains with me. Later that evening I cry and cry and cry saying over and over, "I will never see her again, I will never see her again." My sister tries her best to console a grief that is inconsolable.

The following morning - Monday - heralds another day of awakening to the realisation of the trauma of Tonie's disappearance. New implications have arisen in my mind. I hear undercurrents of conversation between the people around me and the name of David Kelly is mentioned. Instantly, I see in my mind's eye Tonie standing in the kitchen, two months earlier, newspaper spread across the worktop, reading intently an account of the circumstances and death of Dr. David Kelly. He was a government scientist caught up in the tangle of Tony Blair's policy-making relating to the war on Iraq. I gather there had been detailed descriptions of David Kelly's death in some papers and that he had chosen a means to death which would be least painful. This would be to take co-proxomal to dull the pain, then cut the main arteries in the wrists with a sharp knife. I feel nauseous, Tonie is such a gentle person. Would she use a knife on herself? Was she thinking about suicide in July, at the time of David Kelly's death? Perhaps the sudden and unexpected death of a close friend of ours around that same time had affected her badly. Had Jim's death had more of an impact on her than I had perceived? She didn't cry at the funeral, nor did she say much about it other than she was angry that Jim would not talk about his impending death; that there was no opportunity to say goodbye because he behaved right to the end as though death were not imminent. Alas, I will never know. All is speculation, the mind cycles its weary way through all these possibilities, never reaching the end of the road.

With my sister I spend the day sorting out the practicalities of closing the business, not least organising storage for all the books, equipment and furniture. I find I have a strength and clarity of mind to complete these practicalities in the midst of my trauma. I wonder how I can think so clearly on one level and be in such turmoil at another. I have a strong sense of an aura of concern, love and prayer from those around me. Perhaps this is part of the reason I am coping.

Mountains of cards drop through the letterbox. Each card is important, and gives me support and strength when I am so vulnerable. Kate, a friend and professional colleague, arrives; she has been away for the weekend and has just heard of Tonie's disappearance. I am glad of her company and her willingness to be around when my sister leaves tomorrow. Tomorrow would be Dad's birthday if he were alive. He died in January 1992. Will Tonie be found on his birthday?

Tuesday, memories of Dad and his birthday come to mind. It is almost four days now since Tonie walked out of our home. The day is spent packing boxes and making arrangements for their storage. I talk to the landlord and give in my notice on the tenancy of our business property. Part way through the day I feel very tired and my sister and friends tell me to go home for an hour or so.

When I get in I rest for a short time, have something to eat and then prepare to leave. Just before I do I decide to strip the bed my sister has been using and put the sheets in the washing machine. Pulling the sheets back, I see her heated hairbrush still on and just beginning to scorch the bottom sheet. Like the rest of us she is in a state of shock and absent-mindedness. I am so thankful that it crossed my mind to put the sheets in the washing machine. If I hadn't I might have lost my home as well. I interpreted this incident as a further affirmation that God was taking care of me, I felt that I had been prompted to think about washing the sheets and thus discovered a situation, which could have led to another trauma.

I go back to help with the packing but I do not mention the hairbrush, as I know it will upset Jenny. Mick, Jenny's husband, comes to give a hand towards the end of the day and then to take my sister back down south. The three of us arrive home early in the evening to have a meal together, and we find that there is a message on the answer phone from a member of Tonie's family. I cannot believe this. It is just too much. How is it that her estranged family should pick up the news that Tonie is missing, as soon as it goes public? I feel sure that I cannot deal with any of her family, with whom she has had no contact for years. I am both angry and emotionally swamped by this development. Jenny and Mick try to calm and soothe me, as I cry and rant and rave.

Later that evening, Kate comes round to stay with me when my sister and her husband leave. We sit together talking over the events, and the telephone contact from Tonie's estranged family. At 10.30 p.m. the door bell rings. Who can this possibly be at this time of the night? Kate says she will go to the door. She returns, looking worried and pale, and says it is one of Tonie's brothers and his wife. I go to the door. They ask to come in to talk to me; without hesitation I refuse. I know this is one aspect of the tragedy I cannot handle, they must deal with the situation through the police or between themselves. I convey this to them and they leave.

Early on Wednesday morning my brother arrives, and helps me to finalise the return of fees to the parents. Then we meet with friends to clear the business premises and put everything into storage.

The police come and discuss developments and procedures, and it is mooted that a fuller search needs to be carried out by local volunteers. While the police talk at length with me, my brother says he is going for a walk along the canal. When he returns he is smiling. He tells me that as he was walking along the canal he saw a kingfisher, the first he had ever seen. The kingfisher was continually flying ahead of him. Eventually, Harry said he had to stop following it as time was getting on, but he looks at me in a meaningful way. Tonie had said many years previously that once she had seen a kingfisher she would be ready to die. It had become a joke between us that we referred to on the rare occasions that we had sight of this bird. At the time of Tonie's death kingfishers made more than one appearance.

Harry sets off home and Kate offers to ring round the many people Tonie and I know to ask for help with the search the police are organising for Saturday. Later in the evening, there is yet another message on the answering machine from Tonie's brother, in a tone I find threatening and unwelcome. It leaves me distressed and angry.

Kate stays overnight, as by now I am beginning to feel the physical effects of the shock on my system. Having closed the business, as far as I can

I seem more able to let the impact of what has happened penetrate my emotions and consciousness. Kate and I talk at length and decide that it would be a good idea to get away for a while, since the pressure from Tonie's estranged family is too much. In addition, the arrangements for the search are going to make the event more public and there will be inevitable attention from the media. Such attention is welcome from the point of view of maximising the public response for further sightings of Tonie, but unwelcome from my point of view as an individual, caught up in an unexpected and unwanted emotional nightmare.

I arrange with my brother and his wife to travel up North to their home the next day to stay with them for a while. Kate offers to drive the one hundred and thirty mile journey. Up to now I have been driving locally, but I know that my concentration is beginning to slip away, and my ability to remain focused is weakening, so I am glad of her offer.

It is Thursday morning and I finalise the practicalities that need sorting out before I go away. Shortly after lunch the police ring to say that Tonie's disappearance has attracted media attention and I am likely to have to 'face the camera'. They advise me how to deal with the situation. Since I am packed and ready to go to stay with my family, I suggest to Kate that we leave sooner rather than later; perhaps then I will not have to deal with the press. Quickly, we pack Kate's car and take our leave. Just as we are leaving the road from my house, we notice at the T-junction where the road joins the lane, there are two people stopping cars entering our road, "Oh no," I groan. Kate says nothing and keeps driving forward. Fortunately, two or three people turn into the road at the same time, so the reporters (as they turn out to be) have to step back to let us out and the other cars in. We turn out into the lane, Kate puts her foot down on the accelerator. I breathe a sigh of relief as well as experiencing a sense of elation at missing the glare of the media by a hair's breadth. We stop for a short time at Kate's house. I feel a little like a fugitive, on the run from the pressure of the press and Tonie's family.

Travelling to my brother's home via the motorway is a frightening experience, I have the physical sensation that Kate's car is unstable. Although Kate is driving safely and within the speed limits, the speed and movement of the car feels greater than it actually is. This sensation is another manifestation of the effect of shock on my physical and mental being. It is a relief to arrive at our destination. Later that evening while sitting having a meal with my family the first major reaction to the events of the past six days overtakes me, all of a sudden I pick up the plate I am eating from and smash it down onto the table. I am splattered with food. I start screaming and crying uncontrollably. Harry and Ruth come and stand by me, they hold me gently and gradually calm me down. My nephew a young man in his early twenties, sits quietly and looks on wide-eyed at this outburst. Screaming and sobbing violently were to become the two main characteristics of my early grieving pattern.

September 26th 2003

Today – Friday – I wake up in my brother's house. Almost a week has passed since I arrived at my own home last Friday evening, to find Tonie gone. Yes, gone, never to return. The grief is indescribable. I hold her photograph close to me, and know that this is as near as I shall ever be to her again in this world. I just cannot believe this is happening.

Practical demands push me forward. Ruth and Harry go off to work and I gradually get myself together and go into town. I sit in a coffee shop and watch the world go by. It all seems so normal out there, but my inner world is so far from normal. I pick up some cable connections for my computer and return to my brother's house. Then I have a long discussion on the phone with Grant who monitors and maintains my computer. I ask him to take away our business page from the web. I am horrified to find that yet another member of Tonie's family, this time a brother from abroad has, through our web page, made contact by email. I am very angry that Tonie's estranged family should come on the scene. I just cannot cope with them. I realise that they have their own agenda but my feelings towards them are very strong. They couldn't sort out their relationship with Tonie when she was alive, so I cannot even begin, or want to begin, to sort it out in death. There are some things in life that you know you cannot take on board and this, for me, is one of them.

My sister-in-law is working a mile or so away. In the middle of the afternoon, I walk down to see her to have a chat. The short walk leaves me exhausted, and I feel as though my physical resources are fast running out. Ruth notices my exhaustion so she takes me back to the house by car. I haven't been in long when the police ring. They explain that the public search for Tonie, planned for tomorrow, is off. Instead a specialist team of people with dogs is going to carry out the search. This will be more efficient, I am told. The team is the same group of people and dogs who were brought in to help search for Dr. David Kelly. Never in my wildest imagination could I have conceived, back in July, that my life would have any connection, no matter how tenuous, with this government scientist. I feel hopeful that perhaps this team will discover Tonie's body, yet I am still doubtful.

In much of a blur the next few days pass. I continue to sort out practical matters. The police keep in touch by phone but there is little new information surfacing. The search revealed nothing. It is as I thought, Tonie does not want to be found. She could be anywhere. Gradually, as the days pass I feel my physical strength slowly returning. I keep eating during the day and drinking some brandy each night before going to bed, and this seems to help me keep a grip on my general well-being. I am certainly sleeping, and how welcome that sleep is to shut out the nightmare of each day, when in my mind I go over and over all of the recent events.

I decide I will try and write a resume of Tonie's life from when I first knew her until her sudden disappearance, so that I can give this to the police and also share it with my friends and family. My family are the first to read it and they comment on its clarity, saying they do not know how in the midst of this trauma I can write so clearly and logically. I do not know myself. I have a chat with my two nephews and my niece. They are so gentle, understanding and caring, it gives me strength.

On the evening of Friday 3rd, October, Harry and Ruth drive me home. Being away for a short time has helped me and their concern, understanding and kindness has brought me through another week. But I want to be back in my own place. Arriving home I experience the twofold reality of peace and heartbreak, the light and the shade of my predicament. Ruth and Harry stay overnight, but before going to bed we have a bite to eat and they say they will have a glass of brandy. Duly, I produce a brandy for each of them and they are aghast at the amount of brandy in each glass, they only want a third of this amount! I had given them the same quantity as I had been taking each night. They remark that it is no wonder I have been sleeping. For a person who does not normally drink, the volume I have been consuming would surely knock me out. We laughed. Though I felt so sad, I could not help but see the funny side of this situation.

I tell myself on awakening the next day, Saturday morning, 4th October, that life has to go on and I have to get used to living alone and in my new situation. My brother and sister-in-law take their leave. They are having a few days away. I spend the day writing letters and speaking to friends on the phone. In between times, I find myself wandering around the house crying, going in and out of Tonie's room, looking at her empty bed. This was the last place I saw her as she pulled the duvet over her head when I had popped in to say goodbye before going off to work. She had mumbled something in return. Now I scream and scream and call out to an empty house, "How could you? How could you do this?" Sobbing uncontrollably, I feel broken inside, I feel that all the love I gave her, the trust I had in our relationship, the years of working, praying and living together are just nothing, nothing at all. Everything, everything has gone.

I walk into my room and look at the box of co-proxomal in the drawer. I suffer from a back problem and have the medication for when I have a bad bout of pain. I count them. There are about fifty. I wonder how many you have to take to end your life. What is the point of living? How could Tonie give up on our life together? I know I have given my best to Tonie, even though my best, at times, was not up to much. How can this have happened when we got on so well, when we rarely argued, when we shared all we had and each of us was always willing to listen to the other? The many times we laughed together and looked forward to the same things. All my belief in the words that 'love overcomes all things' seems absolutely empty. Love doesn't work, I say to myself, this event has disproved everything I live by and believe in. What is the point of carrying on living when the love you have given isn't good enough? I feel a desperate sense of failure and yet I cannot think what else I could have done. My mind goes back again to that Friday morning on September 19th.

On that morning, I had got up around seven to make myself a drink, to find that Tonie had left a note in the kitchen asking me to cancel her lessons for that day as she felt really ill. I was glad I was up at this time, I knew I would be able to contact the families at home before they set off for work and school. After cancelling her appointments I went to clean out and feed her rabbits. If she was feeling so ill I knew she would not have the energy for this. I decided not to disturb her until around 11.00 am, since it was likely that she would have gone off to sleep as so often happens when she has not slept well during the night. Around half past ten Tonie came into the kitchen. I turned to look at her, she appeared washed out and weary, she said, "I feel dreadful. I am in pain all over my body. I just do not know what to do with myself." I looked at her with a sense of complete helplessness. Over the past four years we had tried every avenue of conventional medicine and alternative therapies to find a solution to the problem of her Chronic Fatigue Syndrome and its unpredictable effects; one minute she is fit and well and the next she is ill and exhausted. I thought about how only three weeks earlier we were in North Yorkshire, walking, talking, watching birds, just enjoying being together. At that time Tonie had easily, at the end of a day climbed 120 steps from the promenade at Scarborough onto a cliff walk, as we made our way back to the town and the car park. I had been amazed on that day; she seemed to have more energy than me.

Then, on that Friday morning, Tonie was pacing around irritated and in pain. I had gently said to her, "It is just something you have to work through till it passes off again, there isn't anything else we can do."

With that, Tonie decided to go for a bath. I continued preparing the lunch. Tonie had not been eating much the last day or two, and on Thursday evening at work, while she was waiting for me to write up my notes and complete my lesson preparation she had said that she was bored. I didn't take much notice of the comment, but I did think it was strange since she was not the sort of person who ever talked of being bored. I was thinking about this, and wondering as I prepared the lunch whether or not she would want to eat anything. After her bath she reappeared, looking much better and brighter and had said, "I'll just order that new maths computer program I was talking about, and do the cheques. Will you pay the cheques in for me at the Post Office on your way to work?"

"Of course I will. Do you want any lunch?"

"No, I'm not hungry."

"Well I will leave you some food in the fridge so if you feel like it a little later you can cook it."

"Okay."

A short time later I went into the lounge, and Tonie said to me, "Ann, will you shred this little cash book when you go to work I don't need it any more". Then she showed me a small sheet of paper and said, "On the first page of this book I had the details of our business account and other information that we both need to know, so I have torn it out. Where should I put it so that you know where it is if I am not around?"

"Oh, just in the drawer there for now … anyway," I said light heartedly, "I don't know why you are worrying about me knowing where it is because we are more than likely to die together in a car crash at this stage in our lives. We are always together and we haven't any life-threatening illnesses!"

"I am going to put it on the front page of this file where I keep all the other accounts, will you remember that?"

"Yes. That's fine."

"I think I'll go back to bed now."

"Okay, I'll have my lunch and get off earlier so that I can go to the Post Office as well." Tonie went off to bed and I ate my dinner and washed up. Then before going to work I popped into Tonie's room and said to her, "I'm off now, but I will try and get home early." Normally Tonie would have turned over to look at me and say goodbye, but that Friday she didn't, she just pulled the duvet over her head and mumbled.

That was the last time I spoke to her, some of my last images are of her stood at the kitchen door looking weary, then in her pink nightie in the lounge discussing where she should put the page from her notebook with all the banking information I would need. At that point I remember thinking how much better she looked than when she had first got up, and wondering why she was bothering about this sheet of paper when I was trying to prepare a meal and get ready for work.

Now two weeks later, I am re-visiting those last hours blaming myself for not having noticed that something was amiss. I recall how ill she looked when she got up, and reproach myself for not having said something more comforting than reminding her the problem was something she had to live with as best she could. Should I have told her instead that I loved and cared about her, might this have made her feel less alone with her Chronic Fatigue? I wish I had gone into her bedroom to see how she was, rather than waiting for her to get up. Was she lying in bed hoping I would come and ask her if she was okay? Did she think I didn't care about how she felt because I hadn't gone in to enquire? I torture myself with thoughts of what I should have done.

Then, I think again of how much better she looked after her bath, she was almost bright and perky. She made the telephone call to order the maths computer program and had a perfectly normal conversation with the recipient of her call. She entered data onto the account sheets and prepared the cheques and the paying-in slip for me to take to the Post Office. I think about how she looked when she was persisting about me knowing where to find the bank details. Her eyes seemed clear and bright and she looked directly at me. Was she thinking to herself that I didn't have a clue about the state of her mind, that her plans were going exactly as she had hoped? Or did she, at that moment, not know herself that in a few hours she would have decided she couldn't bear living with her inner demons any longer? Again and again I replay those last hours in my mind and read over the notes left behind, searching for answers to my many questions.

October 6th 2003

How true the saying is that 'time waits for no-one'. It is Monday October 6th and I am into my third week of waiting. The feeling of depression is taking hold of me so I make an appointment to see my doctor. The last appointment of the day is my slot. Talking to my G.P. I sob, explain how I feel, my doubts and my fears. She tries to re-assure me that there is nothing I could have done to stop Tonie taking her life, that once a person reaches that point nothing and no one can prevent it happening. I wish it could have been prevented. I ask her for some anti-depressant tablets as I feel I am slipping into a reactive depression that is too strong to overcome solely by positive thinking.

I had experienced some months of depression in my mid twenties, due to stress and genetic disposition - there is a leaning towards depression in my father's family. However, after that experience I learnt to control the amount of work and pressure I took on and did not have a further recurrence until my fifties. This time it turned out to be the effect of an undetected, underactive thyroid problem. I recall that period of time; how there were days when I had the urge to drive my car into a wall because I felt so ill, drained and empty and I could not understand why, since there were no external or psychological reasons to explain my problem. I would go to bed at night feeling fine, then awake in the middle of the night feeling incredibly low. I kept telling my doctor that there was something physically wrong with my body, there were hormonal changes taking place, over which I had no control, that were causing this terrible feeling. I also experienced mood swings during the day. One minute I would feel fine, the next minute de-motivated, without energy, depressed. I was fortunate that she had listened to me, and had sent off a blood sample to be tested for evidence of thyroid trouble. The tests came back positive, but it took almost two years of taking thyroxin and anti-depressants for my endocrinal system to get back to normal. Dwelling upon my own experience of depression, and reading around the problem of depression has given me some inkling into one aspect of Tonie's illness. The contrast in the experience seems to be that she did not or could not take steps to discuss and prevent her depression, or to control her urge towards self-destruction.

My G.P. is of the opinion that the shock of the events surrounding Tonie's death have resulted in symptoms similar to post-traumatic stress. After an hour's consultation I am comforted by the doctor's willingness to give her time to listen and advise me and to give me a course of anti-depressants to help me through this difficult period. I am still crying as I leave the surgery, my eyes are swollen, and my head feels heavy. The waiting room is empty; the receptionist is sitting behind the desk, her face glum. No doubt she didn't expect to have to sit there until 7.30 p.m. I get into the car and cry all the way home.

Earlier today I had been for acupuncture with the hope that it would help my body deal with the shock. Laura suggests that massage might be better for me than acupuncture and puts me in touch with Lynn. Lynn is a clinical masseur who sees clients with sports injuries; muscle problems resulting from physical disabilities and people like myself facing emotional traumas or stress. I make an appointment to see her next Wednesday 15th October.

Dreary days drag on. Thoughts move wearily through my mind. The depression is not improving and I increase my medication. I meet with Nathan and on this occasion he suggests that perhaps I should consider the possibility that Tonie may have hidden some things from me, that maybe she is alive somewhere and has gone off to start a new life, that she has made contact with her birth family and so on. I find such thoughts excruciating and yet I must consider the possibility. It is an avenue of investigation that has not been ruled out by the police. Since I didn't detect anything amiss on the day of her departure, then perhaps I need to think this over.

Driving away from Nathan's house I start sobbing and screaming violently. As I cry and scream, I think about how I can possibly be driving safely in this state, though somehow I do. Over the next few weeks I find myself on more than one occasion crying and screaming as I am driving along. It is like a sudden inner explosion that just happens; it is never planned.

Arriving home I get out all the telephone bills for the past six months, recording the calls made from our business number and our home number, I spend hours and hours identifying them all. There are none that seem strange, or that appear to be linked with her birth family as had been suggested might be the case. Tonie had said on numerous occasions that she did not want any contact with her family, as any efforts she had made to build up any meaningful relationship had always ended in an emotional disaster.

Her feelings in this regard were so strong that she made it clear, on more than one occasion, that when she died she did not want her family coming to her funeral. She remarked that they had no interest in her while she was alive, so they need not be present for her death. Her feelings were so strong, that at the time we made our wills she had asked for her wishes to be included in her will, but the solicitor advised her against it. Subsequently she told me that if she died before me, I was not to let her family know of her death. As events turned out I could not carry out her wishes, and this dilemma added to an already fraught situation when that time came.

The police inform me they have had contact with Tonie's estranged family and followed up any leads from them as to where they think she might have gone. I know she has gone nowhere. Her family know nothing about her to give the police any relevant information, their knowledge is ten or twenty years out of date!

I think again about the trainers, and the clothes she was wearing, also the tablets and the knife. These are the only things missing. Her chequebook and cards are all at home and no withdrawals have been made from any accounts. I am not even sure that she has taken a small amount of cash with her. There are posters of her face all around my locality, her name is on the missing persons database. When I look at those posters, I realise I actually blank my thoughts and emotions. I glance at them, but I don't read them. I look at them as though Tonie is a stranger, someone else. She isn't missing I think, she is dead. Perhaps I am wrong though, perhaps I do not know her as well as I think I do.

My friends continue to walk the canal hoping that somewhere a clue might be found that will reveal her whereabouts. Ian has been along the canal numerous times and like my brother has had sightings of a kingfisher, which hitherto he had not seen. The kingfisher and the canal seem to be clues to her whereabouts, but really they are of no help or of any investigative significance. Tonie had been sighted at the end of the road by Vince, and by two ladies getting off the bus. The bus driver did not recognise Tonie from the photograph he was shown by the police and could not recall anyone getting on the bus at that stop. Did she intend getting on the bus and then change her mind because there were people about? I don't know and I will never know. Later in the day she was sighted by a couple walking along the canal towpath. They said they spoke to her but she did not reply, she just looked through them.

On the 13th of October I go for my first massage. Lynn suggests that she uses Neroli oil as this is noted for its properties in helping with grief. The massage shows just how much tension is in my muscles, and even Lynn's light pressure is painful. At the end of the one and a half hour session I realise how much of the shock and tension generated in the last three weeks has made its way into my muscles, and that I am beginning to 'stiffen up'. I find that the massage relieves the tension, and the tears. I decide that I will continue with this therapy as it releases the tension from my mind and muscles. Regular massage could well help prevent muscle and joint problems arising from the shock of Tonie's disappearance and death. I make a further appointment.

My nephew arrives around lunchtime. He suggests we walk along some of the further reaches of the canal; that we start walking from near to where I think Tonie was last seen, and we go on from there. I realise that this is the first time I have been out looking for Tonie since the Friday night she went missing. I have been in such a state of shock, and dealing with so many other things, that it has never occurred to me to go out looking for her myself.

As we walk along together Matt shows remarkable insight into Tonie's character, even though he has not had extensive contact with her. His comments make so much sense. He agrees with me that Tonie would not have put herself in the canal if she didn't like water, and also if she had had a bath before leaving then she is unlikely to have wanted to get dirty. "From what I know of her," he says, "and the nature of her illness, she will have taken the line of least resistance. She will have left the canal path at some point and hidden herself away somewhere."

We walk for some time and see no one. Matt says if anyone saw her, who has not been aware of the appeal for sightings, it is likely that they might have seen her between 5 p.m and 6.30 p.m. This is when people come home from work and go out with their dogs or go for a jog to shake off the stresses of the day.

Walking along Matt points out places where she may have gone. "Look, there is a good gap in this hedge, it leads into a wide field, and there are haystacks over there where she may have hidden between or behind." We walk over to the haystacks. Questions zip through my mind. What state will she be in by now if she is here? How decomposed will her body be? What will we do if we find her? How will I cope? But there is nothing. We look between the trunk of an old tree and the hedge; someone has been there and left behind a piece of clothing.

We continue on, then notice, on the opposite bank of the canal, some old wooden shacks approached by a rickety bridge spanning the canal. We cross the bridge and search around but again find nothing. I tell Matt how I wish I had said something different to her when she came into the kitchen that last Friday morning, told her I loved her and that things would come right eventually. Matt replies, "It wouldn't have made any difference at that stage even if you had told her you loved her, as soon as you had left the house she would have forgotten as her mind would not have been rational, her view of her world and our world on that day was distorted."
I rejoin, "Perhaps, but I would have felt more comfortable with myself, if only I had known how low and depressed she was feeling. She had not indicated that at all, she had only talked about having pain all over her body." We fall silent and

carry on walking. I tell myself I couldn't be a mind reader, yet how I wish I could have read her mind, preventing this tragedy.

Around 4.30 p.m a jogger comes towards us. We stop him, show him Tonie's photograph, tell him she is missing and ask if he can recall having seen her. He shakes his head. I am getting tired by now and suggest that we start walking back, but Matt wants to press on a little further. By five o'clock we have reached a place known as Vimy Ridge. We had been here only a few months earlier with Kate, watching for a barn owl. There are a number of old farm buildings, and a little copse. Matt suggests we search this place more thoroughly, as this would appear to be the furthest most point she could possibly have reached. We spend about half an hour looking around. During this time I notice that several people are coming along this section of the canal, either walking their dogs or jogging. Perhaps I should put her photograph up along this stretch of the canal asking if anyone has seen her, but there is no need.

The following day at around 7.00 p.m. the phone rings. It is Neill. In a cautious tone he says, "There has been a development." He needn't say another word. I know they have found her. He reports that a body has been found which they believe to be Tonie's and the forensic team are at the site of recovery. However, it cannot be said without doubt that it is Tonie until hair samples are matched and dental records checked. Neill says he will need from me details of her dentist, I say I will find them. It is likely to be several hours before it can be confirmed that the body is without doubt Tonie's. It turns out later, when I know

43

where she has been found that Matt and I had started walking along the canal away from the point where Tonie had actually left the canal towpath to find the place where she would lie down and die. We were so near, and yet so far.

Neill notifies my friends of what has happened and they come to be with me. It is twenty-seven days since Tonie went missing, and it would seem that she had walked the canal, following the kingfishers, and looked for a place as Matt had suggested, where she could lay down undisturbed and let her life flow back to its source.

17th October 2003

Neill arrives first thing this morning to collect the name and location of Tonie's dental practitioner so that the police can acquire her dental records. It is hoped that once they have Tonie's dental records for matching, the pathologist will complete the formal identification. Neill says he will be back later for me to identify some items that were found by Tonie's body.

The items are brought. With gentleness and sensitivity Neill asks if I am ready to look at them. I nod. Opening the plastic bag he takes out her watch, the empty pill bottle and the knife. The watch is Tonie's, the knife is from our kitchen and the pill bottle - well it must be from here, even though there is no label to indicate this; what was missing from her room was the box of co-proxomal, so I can only think that she put the pills into this bottle. Neill points out that the knife has not been used, and the recovery of her body by the forensic team confirms this fact. That is a relief. It appears that she overdosed on the tablets and allowed them to take their effect, but further tests have to be conducted before a fuller picture will emerge of how many tablets she took, and how much they contributed to her death. I am puzzled that her spectacles, her slippers, and the thicker coat she took with her are missing. She must have discarded them as she walked along; perhaps they were too heavy to carry. Looking at the items there on the table, I feel terribly, terribly sad as I dwell on the emotional and mental pain she must have been going through. What an ending to a life of someone so caring, gentle, intelligent, witty and full of laughter ...

Neill removes the items from the table and puts them back in the plastic bag. I sense he is relieved that this task is over. I ask if I can have her watch, he says that I will be able to have it eventually but, like the notes she had written, these items are police property when someone has taken their own life, they are part of the 'evidence'. Suicide still bears characteristics of the criminal offence it was in Great Britain until 1961, and as recently as 1993 in Ireland; evidence is gathered, examined, then the results brought to a conclusion in the courtroom, albeit a Coroner's Court.

It is late afternoon when Neill comes to take Kate and me to the place where Tonie's body was recovered. I sit in the front of the police car feeling numb, physically present to the world around me, but mentally in my own distressed, painful inner world. A few minutes drive down the lane, Neill pulls the car to an abrupt halt commenting that someone is tailgating him. I immediately think it is a member of Tonie's family, and this thought makes me realise how vulnerable and harassed I feel at the behaviour of one of her brothers, who, from my viewpoint, has a particularly aggressive manner. When Neill returns to the car, I am relieved to know my fears are unfounded.

I am unfamiliar with the route we take out into the countryside but eventually we arrive at a farm gate. Neill pulls the car off the road and we get out.

Together, Neill, Kate and I walk into the field and follow what appears to be both a public footpath and a farm track. As we approach the place of Tonie's death, Kate remarks that there are skylarks singing. We look towards the source of the song and sure enough, just close by, the larks are rising from the field into the sky. Then we stop by a hedge. Neill points to a ditch at the other side of the hedge saying, "That is where she was found." We peer through a hole in the lower part of the hedge, but I do not feel near enough.

"Can I go round into the field?"

"Do you really want to?"

"Yes."

"Actually it is private land, but I know the owner so it will be okay."

Kate and I follow Neill back down the track. We walk through a gap between the hedge and the fence of an adjacent field, then continue along the edge of the field and the ditch. Neill points to the rubber glove the forensic team tied to the hawthorn branch overhanging the ditch to mark the place where she was found. I stand and stare at the empty ditch, trying to picture her decomposed body. I jump down; I want to stand at the actual place of her death.

On the way to the field Neill told me that, as we had discussed a week or so earlier, it was dogs that had located her body. A local man who walked the path twice a day with his dogs had noticed that they had gone through the gap in the hedge and were engrossed with something in the ditch. To his shock he thought that what he saw was a decomposed body and he had quickly notified the police.

Stepping out of the deep ditch, I ask Neill if I can talk to the person who found her. Neill says he will go and enquire, as the man lives close by. Kate and I stand together quietly with our own thoughts, waiting. Neill returns with Bob. Bob and I walk away from Neill and Kate. I thank him for finding Tonie and being willing to talk to me. I express my concern at what effect finding her body has had on him. He tells me that it was a great shock, but fortunately he has been at the scene of accidents in his younger days so that in some ways he was prepared to deal with the sight that met his eyes. I am anxious to tell him about Tonie. I do not want him left with the image of a decomposed body, but to know something of Tonie when she was alive. We talk together for a while and then go our separate ways.

GRIEF is the only word I write in my notebook today, Saturday October 18th 2003. Anguish racks my entire being. I am distressed that I came away from the ditch without having said a prayer, without carrying out some ritual to help me come to terms with Tonie's death, to make holy a death, which may be thought in some ways as unholy. Thinking this over, I decide to make contact with Colin, a priest and friend, and ask him if he can come with me, my friends and family to the ditch tomorrow, and there pray with us for Tonie. He says he will be able to make it for about four o'clock in the afternoon. Neill obtains permission from the owner of the field for us to go there at this time.

The nights are beginning to draw in. It is still light when we arrive at the field. I am comforted that Neill has come along. It could well be his day off, but he cares enough to be here. I am struck by how smart he is, that he has taken trouble with his appearance, his shoes gleam and he looks as though he has just stepped out of the shower.

Colin's face is serious, yet his eyes and his manner communicate compassion. In his hands he bears a prayer book and the holy water. Together, we all walk to the ditch in the field. We gather round Colin to pray, Neill stands at a distance and I feel a sense of his presence guarding us, giving dignity and respect to Tonie's death and to our time of prayer and blessing.

Colin expresses the thought that, while we bless the ground (on which Tonie died) with holy water, she had already blessed it with her body and that the sprinkling of holy water is an acknowledgment and respect for Tonie's life and death, not an act of cleansing the ground as would have been the purpose in the past. I am thankful for this priest's wisdom, his compassion and insight into the dilemma of death by suicide in the twenty-first century. We pray together, and bury deep in the earth a small crucifix to represent our belief that in all circumstances Christ is with us in our suffering and death. We proclaim our faith that God was with Tonie in her death, he did not desert her in her anguish and distorted perception of reality, neither will he desert us through our anguish and our tears.

When our prayer is complete, the light in the sky is fading, the air bears a November chill, we pull our coats around us and keep close to each other. Silently, we walk away from the ditch, I lean on my brother's shoulder and sob uncontrollably. At this moment the light of Tonie's presence in my life is fading away and the frosty winds of anguish and grief make their presence felt in my inner spirit.

Within a few days of Tonie's body being recovered, I am informed that she had taken an overdose of paracetamol but further tests have to be conducted to establish a clearer picture of the amount of paracetomol/co-proxomal she had taken. Once the necessary samples have been taken for analysis, her body will be released for burial. I am also told that Tonie's brother who has been harassing me, has been trying to gain access to her remains. It seems he is of the opinion that because he is 'family' he believes he has the right to claim her in death and organise her funeral.   I find this problem an added strain to an already traumatic situation. How glad I am that Tonie had always insisted that we had a will, and told me that if we did not have a will I would have nothing but trouble from her family. In the event, of her seven brothers and sisters, it was just one member of her family who caused a problem, while paradoxically another member of her family showed me concern, compassion and understanding. Once the Coroner's Office had sight of her will, they were able to inform Tonie's brother that he had no rights in relation to Tonie's remains, or her funeral arrangements. That said, I find myself left with this situation where I recognise that however distant and estranged her birth family, they are aware of her death and its circumstances, and they have their own thoughts and needs. I wrestle to find an answer to what seems to be an implacable problem – meeting the demands of the living and the dead.

Finally, I come to the conclusion that the best way forward is to arrange a private funeral for Tonie to which her family will be able to come, and a memorial service for my family, and for all our friends, clients and colleagues.

I ask Jean to go with me to choose a coffin and to make arrangements at the funeral directors. We sit together in the room set aside for discussing such matters, and all the while it seems unreal. Here we are, talking in a perfectly normal way, discussing the price of coffins, hearses, and cremation fees, yet my life is anything but normal. There is one part of me walking, talking, speaking, and another part of me detached from the action. It is almost as though I am watching myself perform all these actions. I suppose it is the effect of shock.

Monday evening 3rd November 2003. I stand at an open door, gazing out into the night. The cold air brushes across my face as I watch the hearse reversing into the courtyard; lights from the chapel and those in the courtyard give off a soft light, conveying a mood of gentleness to my heavy heart. Tonie's funeral is taking place in a small convent chapel away from the city, at a place she loved and with a community of sisters whom we both know and tonight her body is being received into the church. I look at the coffin in the hearse, and find myself saying inwardly 'Tonie's skeleton is in that coffin, her physical presence has gone forever, I will never see her smile again, or share her laughter or ...' We start singing:

> The hand of God shall hold you,
> The power of God enfold you,
> The love that dreamed and formed you,
> Still surrounds you here today;
> The light of God beside you,
> Above, beneath, inside you,
> The light that shines to guide you home
> To the loving hand of God[6]

I feel the presence of my close friends and this community united with me in sorrow and in faith. Their love and care strengthen me. Their acceptance of Tonie's way to death, their compassion towards her renews my own faith in the infinite compassion of God. I believe that He has taken Tonie into a new life beyond death, not condemned her to further anguish and torment and taken her into a life of the spirit of which we can only dream. This is now her reality. Just as the earthly life that I shared with Tonie has gone, and our life of reality on earth over, those twenty-two years are now the dream.

Colin conducts this short ceremony with propriety, and assures those of us who are grieving her loss that while Tonie walked on her own to her death, she was never totally alone. God was with her in a way we do not know or understand because He is a God of mercy and compassion, he understood her pain, her weakness, her torment. We place on Tonie's coffin objects symbolising important aspects of her life, we pray together in memory of her, and for ourselves. Later I sit on my own in the darkness of the chapel. The sanctuary light is burning steadily, my hand is on her coffin. I pray for acceptance of this tragic, unwelcome death, for strength to remember the many good and fruitful years we have spent together. But oh, how I am going to miss her companionship, her commitment, and her wit – all those attributes that made Tonie the special person she was to me and to others. There are no words or images that can express the abyss of her loss. I am still in a deep state of shock. I cannot believe that this is the eve of her funeral, even though I know it is. I leave the chapel and make my way to bed. I am staying here with this community for a few days; their love and care will help me through this trauma.

Tuesday 4th November is Tonie's funeral mass, and I will be glad when it is over. Some of Tonie's family have chosen to be at her funeral and I have tried to think of ways to make them part of the service, to allow for their grief. I have also brought photographs of Tonie, letters from people far and wide expressing their condolences on Tonie's death as also their appreciation of her gifts and their special memories of her life. I bring her certificates showing her academic achievements. My purpose, I realise, is to direct those at the funeral to focus on the positive aspects of her life, even though this makes her manner of death seem even more futile. There is no answer to the futility of her death, or any ultimate comfort that makes sense or justifies her means to death, yet there is a need to reach towards this goal, to make some sense out of such a senseless situation.

I brace myself to face Tonie's family, and to be as kind as I can towards them. I cannot mend their relationship with her. I cannot fulfil her wish that they should not be here but I can attempt to put aside my anguish for a few hours and look beyond this moment. Fortunately for me there are many priests at her funeral mass and the Bishops of our diocese. Their presence, their understanding, their prayerful support help me through, as does the presence of the religious community. While I try to behave 'normally' I feel far from normal. I feel as though I am an actor on a stage, playing a role, and that my real self is in the audience, watching the performance. The funeral mass is an endurance. As the service progresses I recall that one of Tonie's sisters has acknowledged my grief and Tonie's request for the family not to be at the funeral and consequently she did not come today. This comforts me, at least someone in Tonie's family seems to understand her. The tears fall slowly and silently down my cheeks as the last hymn is sung. The hymn helps express some of the dimensions of my personal faith and my anguish:

> Be still my soul: the Lord is at your side;
> Bear patiently the cross of grief and pain;
> Leave to your God to order and provide;

In every change he faithful will remain.
Be still my soul: your best, your heavenly friend,
Through thorny ways, leads to a joyful end.

Be still my soul; your God will undertake
To guide, the future as he has the past.
Your hope, your confidence let nothing shake,
All now mysterious shall be clear at last.
Be still my soul; the tempests still obey
His voice, who ruled them once on Galilee.

Be still my soul; the hour is hastening on
When we shall be for ever with the Lord,
When disappointment, grief and fear are gone,
Sorrows forgotten, love's pure joy restored.
Be still, my soul; when change and tears are past
All safe and blessed we shall meet at last.[7]

Before we leave for the crematorium we have lunch. Later the hearse
arrives to take Tonie's remains and a small group of us to the crematorium.
Sitting in the funeral car I gaze in front of me at the hearse moving slowly down
the tree-lined drive guided by the principal undertaker walking ahead with

measured and dignified pace. Once out onto the road, he steps into the hearse and we travel on at driving speed.

I have no idea where the crematorium is situated. I selected it as the nearest one to the location of the funeral mass. The journey feels like miles. I stare out of the windows, looking without seeing, intent on keeping myself together for a few more hours. The cars turn into the crematorium and to my consolation it is an attractive, well-tended oasis of trees, shrubs, flowers and grassy areas. Nathan had offered to conduct the service at the crematorium and he does so now with gentleness and sensitivity. After the prayers and his short but meaningful words, he invites each of us to go up to the coffin and sprinkle it with holy water as a symbol of blessing and of our final farewell to Tonie. I have made a point of standing behind the family, of allowing them to go first. Then I walk out, sprinkle the coffin with holy water and stand a moment to tell myself yet again that Tonie's body is in that coffin, that she has gone from this life. The coffin slips silently and gracefully from view, and we leave the chapel. I stand next to Nathan feeling like a marble statue; lifeless, cold and distant from the present moment. While I stand there I think to myself that I have still to get through the memorial service, which is only two days away.

By the time the 6th November comes, the date arranged for Tonie's memorial service, I feel I am coming to the end of my strength. But this evening is important because it is an opportunity for the children Tonie taught to have their chance to say goodbye. It is a time for my friends, family, parents, pupils, colleagues and others to join together in prayer and remember Tonie's life. I have asked Richard, a priest and friend, to conduct the ceremony. I have selected music and readings from Tonie's Mass of Final Vows in May 1987. On this day Tonie made a life-long commitment to a consecrated life, it was a day filled with joy and promise for our future. I want the children to experience joy and remember Tonie as they knew her, her laughter, her kindness, her willingness to help them to achieve their goals. The service goes smoothly and prayerfully, fragrance from the flowers fills the air, everyone sings, prays, listens, we are united as one in remembering Tonie with love and commending her to God's infinite compassion and care. The children light candles in memory of Tonie, the lights are switched off and in that dimmed church we each have our own thoughts. Then Richard reads the following poem to guide and comfort us:

> You can shed tears that she has gone,
> Or smile because she has lived.
>
> You can close your eyes and pray she will come back,
> Or open them and see all she has left behind.
>
> Your heart can be empty because you can't see her,
> Or full of the love and kindness that you shared.
>
> You can turn your back on tomorrow and live for yesterday,
>
> Or you can take yesterday and transform it tomorrow because of her example.

You can remember her and only that she is gone
Or cherish her memory and let it live on.

You can cry, and close your mind, be empty and turn
your back

Or do what she would want; smile, open your eyes, love
and go on with her safe in your heart.[8]

Presently these words are just sentiments. How long the journey, how many tears before the words can become a day-to-day reality? Will I ever live them? I do not know, for now those sentiments remain in the lifeless ink upon paper, squiggles and patterns forming words waiting to be received into the heart and spirit and brought alive.

After the service I stay at the back of the church to greet some of the four hundred or more people who have come to say goodbye to Tonie. People offer gestures of kindness through their tears, hug me and express their sadness and their concern, I am glad so many people came. Their presence affirms that Tonie was not only very important to me, but that she is cared for enough by others for them to have taken the time to be here tonight.

Friday 7th November. Gerald, another priest, has offered to come to the crematorium to sprinkle the ashes; this is the final act of the meaningful rituals I have been following, but also the last part of the 'public grieving.' I have been trying to be normal in an abnormal situation, but for the most part my outward appearance has not been a reflection of what has been happening to me inwardly and it will be a relief when the ashes have been scattered.

Kate, Ian, Jean, Peter and Lesley accompany me to the crematorium. We meet Gerald and a member of the staff from the crematorium, who carries Tonie's ashes and takes us to the area where they are to be scattered. I walk, my head bowed, looking at the damp grass beneath my feet as I plod towards the designated place. Tears and anguish are rising from the depths of my pain and shock, and cannot be contained, I try to suppress the urge to scream out against this whole event, but I cry gently. I manage to keep the flood of my pain in abeyance while the prayers are said and we sprinkle petals gathered from the flowers out of Jean's garden over Tonie's ashes. Then my emotions take over, in a torrent of violent weeping, I lean in turn on the shoulders of my friends, aware of their own pain and sense of helplessness at my distress. I decide I need to stay awhile at the crematorium. Kate says she will sit with me until I have exhausted my crying, the others leave me reluctantly and with sadness.

Kate and I sit on a bench close to where we have distributed the ashes. My tears seem to come from the very centre of my being, from a place so deep within me that is beyond all telling. Kate sits quietly at my side, speaking when she thinks it will help, silent at other times. We stay until I can cry no more. Although it is only four o'clock, the light is beginning to recede from the sky, as it does at this time of the year. Any warmth from the early winter's sun has gone and the November evening is creeping in. We head for home, one major part of shock and grief lived through, but yet so much still ahead, not least the inquest.

Distinctive to all suicide bereavement is the process of the inquest and the Coroner's Court. I try not to think about it. Tonie's suicide has brought to my door my first encounter with the police, with court procedures and the intrusion of the media into my private life. Until now I have managed with Neill's help to shelter myself from the media, but I am aware that they have the right to be at the Coroner's Court. I just hope there is something more interesting for them today than Tonie's death.

Kate picks me up and we drive into the city and park the car. We arrive at a massive, dreary, black-painted door. The door is as faceless as I would like to be, and as unwelcoming as this place is to me. We press the buzzer to announce our presence and I wonder what lies ahead of me, behind this façade. The door opens and we are in a foyer with stairs ahead of us, towards which we are directed. At the top of the stairs we stand, register our arrival and wait to be instructed to enter the court. I see a member of Tonie's family there and am glad I have asked my solicitor to be present for the proceedings, just in case any unexpected difficulties should arise. I feel extremely vulnerable and am so grateful for those friends who are with me, who act as a shield around me.

The court procedure was not unduly unpleasant, but I was very disappointed with the Coroner. I cannot remember his exact words but he opened the proceedings by saying something like, "Tonie was a nun was she not?" I knew that this was just the sort of thing the press would like to hear. Anyone in a public office, who takes their life, such as doctors, nurses, police, church roles etc., attract more attention from the media than the 'man in the street'. The phrasing used by the Coroner seemed to indicate that he was playing to the reporter present by drawing attention to the fact of Tonie's religious commitment. I consider that he could for example have said, "Tonie was suffering from M.E. or C.F., was she not at the time she went missing?" This would have set a different tone to the inquest and maybe to the reporting.

Immediately after the inquest a reporter, who was brash and pushy, approached me. In some ways I wish I could have spoken to her and had some influence in what was written, but I was still too traumatised, and I had asked my solicitor to keep the media away from me.

In the event Tonie's death was reported by the use of large bold headlines on the inside page of the local paper reading, "MISSING NUN: SUICIDE FEAR." Since open verdict had been the coroner's conclusion I felt the headline was cruel and unfeeling towards those of us who had lost someone so precious and the wording had been chosen merely to sensationalise her death. The mention of the outcome of open verdict was embedded in the general text and I could well imagine it had been passed over by the majority of readers. I was angry, as were my friends, we had expected the report to appear as it does in most cases, as a small entry in a side column with a small heading. One friend wrote a letter of complaint to the newspaper he was so incensed by the nature and quality of the reporting. A comment someone made about this incident that did help at that time was, "Just forget it, newspaper is news today and chip paper tomorrow." How very true that statement is. I took that philosophy on board and let go of the anger.

On reflection I realised that in the totality of Tonie's suicide I had for the most part been able to avoid the media. I had not watched the TV, or listened to the radio when appeals were made. I think it was a form of defence to protect myself from more emotional battering. Needless to say, it was a relief when the inquest was over and any further media intrusion became highly unlikely, I could now turn my mind to other aspects of my bereavement.

Part Two

Reflections

Grief

I imagine that all of you, my fellow sufferers and survivors, identify with some of the following words: gone, shock, disbelief, anger, guilt, grief, anguish, relief, sadness, depression, confusion, preoccupation with the suicidal event and emptiness. They all form, in one-way or another, part of the grief process.

Bereavement has always been a subject, which has interested me, along with the care of the bereaved. My first steps, twenty years or more ago, into learning something of the process of bereavement began with reading the work of Elizabeth Kubler Ross, in her well known book *On Death and Dying*[9] Subsequently I have read many books and articles on the subject, and have shared and experienced bereavement, but none of that prepared me for the impact of Tonie's sudden and tragic death. That reading and experience provided me with knowledge of the various reactions and processes that bereavement brings in its wake. This knowledge has enabled me to talk freely and openly about what was happening to me. There have been times when I might have felt I was going 'mad' had I not known that my reactions and feelings were part of the normal grieving process. I had also come to the conclusion over the previous years that grief does not follow an exact pattern, rather, each person experiences similar characteristics of bereavement that come and go as we try to rebuild our life after the death of someone significant.

The finality of the word GONE can have no greater fullness of expression than in the experience of death. I knew as I read the note Tonie had left, that she was gone forever. 'Gone,' has never embodied such emptiness, such finality. Tonie had gone from my world, never to be seen again in the way I had known, never to be here to complete the earthly dreams we still held together, never to share each other's company, to talk, to laugh, to work, to live together again. Tonie had GONE FOREVER. How did I know that she had gone forever, when she had not said explicitly in her note that she intended to take her own life? I knew, because having arrived at the stage of walking out from our home, leaving a note packed with negative thoughts and feelings, that there was no way she would want to be found alive. I was convinced of this because since her minor attempt at suicide, almost twenty-five years previously, she had made two comments during the ensuing years about others who subsequently died as a result of suicide. On one occasion she had commented, "I sometimes feel like that, but would never do that to you." The other was, "If 'they' want to be successful they should not attempt suicide at home. They should go far away so that they are not found. I feel sorry for these people because they have been brought back into a living hell." At the time of these remarks I now realise that I had thought them 'odd', yet I had taken them as emanating from the light of her own past experience. For example, I did not think that she seriously felt like taking her own life, but that she meant she had had a passing thought about suicide. I also believed without doubt that her sense of belonging and of the meaning of life was complete in the trust, faith and life we shared and that she would never attempt suicide again. How wrong was my conviction? With regard to her comment about people needing to go away from their homes to end their lives, I recalled that she was quite angry and irritable when she talked about this. I remembered thinking at the time, "Why is she so angry?" I reasoned that she felt sorry for those who were unsuccessful in their attempts at suicide, as she knew what a long, hard road it was to recovery. But now I ask myself, was she angry that she was still alive? Did she actually feel suicidal quite often, and why had I not recognised this? More questions adding to the hundreds of others we ask ourselves after we lose someone precious to suicide.

From the moment I read Tonie's note I went into that dual sense of reality and unreality. I engaged in the reality of the practical things that needed doing. For example, on reading Tonie's note I made myself a cup of coffee, then wandered round the house looking for what was missing. I believe the practical necessities help to keep you sane. Yet, at another level, everything was unreal. I was talking to people, but was not present to them. I took in what was going on around me, but was not part of it. I do not know exactly how long I was in this mode of existence, possibly about five to six months, but I do recall when I began to emerge from it. It was on one of the days I had gone for a massage. I was lying there and the ticking of a clock caught my attention. I asked, "Lynn has that ticking clock always been in this room?" "Yes," was her reply. That moment marked the start of slowly becoming present to the physical world around me, rather than passing through it. Moving on from being disengaged from concrete reality, locked in a world of emotional and mental trauma to the process of merging that trauma into my being as a person and with my life experience; to reenter life, to get ready to live without Tonie, to leave the past behind. But what a slow process that is. It requires the help and support of the people around us, along with effort and determination on our part to drag us out of the 'pit' of this experience of 'gone.'

The realisation that Tonie had gone, set in motion a roller coaster of shock and disbelief. How well we survivors know these feelings. I said hundreds of times, "I just can't believe it, I just can't believe it." I had no doubt that Tonie was dead but just could not believe that she had taken her own life. The physical effects of the shock were tension and pain in my muscles, reactive depression and bouts of screaming that I could never have imagined possible. I walked around the house screaming with emotional pain, as though the very centre of my being had been ripped out. I found myself screaming in the car as I was driving and shouting out, "Oh Tonie, Tonie, Tonie." That sense of emptiness was physical. The black hole I spoke of earlier was focused in the solar plexus, at the very centre of my nervous system in the ganglia of tissue and nerves that form part of the autonomic nervous system. The shock, manifesting itself in the nerve centre of my being seemed to produce a chemical reaction, the outcome of which, was causing me to feel depressed.

Everything I looked at in the house was a reminder of Tonie. I screamed and shouted at her, "How could you leave me? How could you?" I threw things at the walls in frustration and pummelled the bed with my fists to expend the frustration I felt at so many unanswered questions, at the futility of the event, of life itself. What is the point? What is the point? The only time I can identify a conscious anger against Tonie was on the day immediately after she had gone. On that Saturday I was angry that she was causing all this fuss by her disappearance; police and public involvement, helicopter searches, distress and anguish to all of us who knew and loved her. Yet, this feeling of anger soon passed and by that same evening I felt only compassion for her and for the suffering she must have been going through and maybe was still enduring wherever she was. Instead of anger, I experienced frustration, which demonstrated itself in the same way as anger. I felt deeply hurt and rejected and cried my soul out from that place within myself, known only to me and felt only by me. That pain which is individual to each of us.

I did, however, realise through my dreams that there was anger within me directed towards her. The most vivid dream relating to that anger was of her returning home. In this dream Tonie walked into the house a month later and was laughing and saying to me how could I even think she would be driven to suicide. She was fed up with me and thought she would go away for a while. In the dream Tonie was acting as though nothing had happened, and seemed totally unable to understand my point of view. I found myself desperately trying to make her understand how devastated I was that I couldn't possibly go on as though nothing had happened. I told her she had made me feel suicidal and that I would do the same to her, then she will know what it feels like! This dream had been preceded the day before by another dream in which I was walking along a street and could see a building on fire. I went in to try and help, but there was nothing but utter devastation, everything was black, burnt and ruined. For me this dream represented how I was experiencing my life at that moment. There are numerous theories about dreams, but one constant theme seems to be that in some way they help us to deal with reality, they can confront some of the thoughts that we will not allow ourselves to face when we are awake, or they present to us in symbolic form events taking place in our lives.

Looking back to those days when I felt I was passing through reality, rather than present to it, I realise that much of the time was spent in reliving the event of the suicide. When Tonie's body was recovered I did not ask to see her remains, as I knew that given the weather conditions since she had gone missing and the period of almost a month, decomposition would be well advanced. Nevertheless, after Tonie's cremation I found myself constantly thinking about the state of her body when she was found and the fact that, in the final event, I hadn't even asked what she had been wearing. I wondered whether I should ask to see the photographs, which I knew would have been taken at the site of the recovery of her body. I looked up details of decomposition on the Internet to confirm what in my heart I knew. This obsession was not to do with disbelief in her death, I believed that from the beginning. My disbelief was to do with the suicide. Even though I knew without a doubt that she had been driven to a self-inflicted death there was a sense of incompleteness because I had not 'seen her dead.' In the event I gradually worked through this issue and decided that it would not help me to look at the photographs or talk to the people who recovered her body because it would not change the fact that she was dead, and dead as a result of being exhausted with life.

Another obsession was the longing to retrieve her ring and her watch, the two items that she always wore and by which I had confirmed her identity. These were in police custody and I remember feeling scared that I would not get them back. I wanted to have something that was part of her when she died. Eventually, I was able to collect the ring and the watch. When I opened the plastic bag in which the two items had been placed, the smell of death rose to my nostrils. The glass was missing from the face of the watch and the expanding bracelet, when it was stretched, revealed her decomposed skin. The smell of the chemicals that must have been used to clean the ring and the watch still clung to them. I washed the ring and placed it on my finger. Then I spent hours and hours cleaning the bracelet with a pin, picking out death trapped between its links. Finally, when I had cleaned it I took the watch to a jeweller to have a new glass over the face and have it restored to working order.   As I walked out of the shop without the watch, I felt as though I was leaving Tonie behind and I could not rest until I had the watch back. Another urge that had to be satisfied was to walk the path she had taken to her death. It was springtime before I did that - six months or more after her death. I bought a pedometer because I wanted to know exactly how far she had walked, and to work out at what point she must have left the canal to arrive in the field where she was eventually found. I had not chosen a specific day. I woke up one morning and decided that was the day I would go.

As I walked along I reflected on some of the information that Neill, the police officer, had given me when they were searching for Tonie. He said that Tonie's personality profile fitted the category of a 'despondent', and these people were frequently found at places where water meets land, where a hedge meets a field or pathway, or at the site of a vista and more often than not close to habitation. And so it was. Tonie lay down in a deep ditch, by a hedge close to a country track with houses backing onto the field a few hundred yards away. On the day I followed in her footsteps the weather was much as it had been on the day she had walked that path; mild and sunny. But no doubt she had been unaware of the beauty of nature around her. She was trapped in that 'unknown' state of mind that we who are left behind try to understand, but cannot, her experience of reality at that moment twisted, crippling and destructive. For myself, I was still in the unreal world of my loss, going over and over the events of September 2003, trying to fill in those final hours of Tonie's life and our life together. All those questions, all that searching consumed my thinking, day and night, as I tried to assuage my relentless need for answers.

Three hours or more after I had left home I came to the point where Tonie must have left the canal. There were two ways she may have gone. One was a path through the wooded hill area, and the other a straight path between two fields. I explored the path through the wood, and recalled Matt's comment that she would have taken the easiest route. The wood was not too dense, but the path was far from clear, there were branches across the path and difficult muddy areas to negotiate. I decided it was unlikely she would have chosen this route, although

I will never know for sure. The path between the fields brought me close to where she was found. It ended at a junction where one could turn right, left, or go straight ahead. The path to the right went into the wood, the path straight ahead led back to the road, and the path to the left was narrow, more hidden and bounded by two high hedges. This seemed the most likely route. I walked along and eventually came to a gate into a field, which was also the entrance to a footpath heading to some houses in the near distance. I turned into the field and saw that ahead there was a vista. Standing at the top of that field you could see for miles. I sat down. Did she sit here? Did she look at this vista? Did she think of coming back home? Did she hope someone would come along and help her? Again, no answers to the endless questions, only possibilities. Perhaps she had sat there for a while and then made her way down the field and slid down into the ditch. I mulled over all these thoughts and decided that I would choose an ending that seemed most likely from what I knew of her. My ending is that she did walk along the track between the fields, that she came up this little lane into this field, and eventually made her way down into the ditch exhausted and desperate and let her life come to an end.

Looking at my watch, I saw I had an hour before the bus was due for my homeward journey. I rose to my feet, retraced my steps to the crossroad of country tracks, then followed the path and the hedge towards the road. Part way along the track I turned in between the hedge and the field to look along the ditch once again, at the rubber glove hanging from the branch. Sadness clothed me as I left the field and walked towards the village, but at the same time I felt I had taken one step nearer to coming to terms with my loss.

Guilt and a sense of responsibility towards Tonie's death were problems to be dealt with. I read more books on the subject of depression, the problem of Chronic Fatigue, talked through my thoughts and feelings with friends and a counsellor. All this, along with my own experience of depression, helped me to accept that I was neither guilty nor responsible for Tonie's death. In fact, shortly after her death a friend had said to me, "Tonie did not lay any blame at your door for her death so you need not do so." That was true. In the note she left she vindicated me of any need to blame myself. Essentially, she could not live with the effects of the Chronic Fatigue and the recurring childhood traumas that had risen up with renewed ferocity. Her sense of helplessness and hopelessness while she was in this vulnerable state had driven her over the edge.

Nevertheless, responsibility towards other people is one of the cornerstones to the successful growth of the family, race, nation and the global community. Without each of us assuming responsibility for others and ourselves, existence would be tenuous. So how can we, as the bereaved survivors of suicide, have no responsibility for the suicide of someone who meant so much to us, or even for a person we may not have liked all that much? The answer for me has been in accepting that I could not take responsibility for the inner life, experience and the effects of illness on Tonie's mental health. These areas of her life were beyond my reach. It is our inner life that makes us individuals, and no matter how much we love someone else, we can only know what they are thinking and feeling by what they tell us. We cannot be guilty of their depression, which is an illness, as is the urge to self-destruct, lying at the far end of a continuum of awful and unimaginable emotional pain. Reading accounts written by those who have suffered the extremes of depression, but have subsequently recovered and written about their experience, I realised that no amount of love from another, no amount of success, no amount of money can assuage that inner desolation. Among the books I have read, since her death, by people who have been close to suicide I found the most moving account in *Darkness Visible*[10] written by William Styron. Styron conveys the utter sense of loss the individual experiences, the compulsion towards self-destruction that cannot be stopped, the feeling that the brain is out of control. He writes, 'of my brain in thrall to its outlaw hormones' and I thought of Tonie's note, where she had written, 'I need to extinguish my mind.' The feelings of self-loathing and hate are there in his writing as it was in Tonie's note. For me, Styron comes the nearest to conveying the unconveyable. It seems to me now that the cocktail of past emotional traumas and illness such as Chronic Fatigue can be ingredients for suicidal illness. I also realised that thousands of people, myself included, have suffered depression but we have never reached this extreme form of the illness. Some people endure the most horrific losses and abuses in childhood, but live with the memories and do not have to erase them through self-destruction. Suicidal illness is so highly complex, and there is so much to learn.

The countless studies and continuing research bears testimony to this fact. I found Kay Redfield Jamison's book on suicide *Night Falls Fast*[11] a help and guide as I sought to come to grips with this whole problem. This author is a Professor of Psychiatry at the Johns Hopkins University in America. She has the remarkable insight of one who has not only experienced the compulsion of suicide, but also treated those suffering from this affliction. It is highly readable, authoritative and a well-researched book.

The only phrase within Tonie's note that I could have taken personally were her words, 'I feel so unloved.' These words were hard to accept not only for me, but also for our closest friends as we all truly loved and cared about her. But gradually I realised that she was not saying that others did not love her, but in her state of mind at that time, in that horrendous hell she was in, she was unable to feel the tremendous love and affection people had for her. This inability to perceive the love of others is another distortion of reality that suicidal illness brings. While I have come to accept that I am not guilty for her death, or responsible, I still wish it could have been different, that I could have known how ill she was feeling. I wish she had been able to tell me, as William Styron had told his wife, that help was needed.

The experience of loss is more than just the loss of the person's presence, personality, love and companionship. It is also the loss of all their many talents and attributes. In Tonie I lost a friend, a person sharing my consecrated life, a business partner, a dressmaker, a decorator and DIY person. In short I felt as though I had lost everything including a part of myself. Losing a part of oneself means the loss of shared memories; those events that only the two of you have experienced, that you can recall, discuss and laugh about. I found the loss of shared memories particularly painful. It is these numerous losses that generates grief and anguish.

For me grief is the sense of loss, and anguish is the pain it brings. I know now that I had no concept of the meaning of these words prior to Tonie's death. I also find it hard to explain, or put into words, that aching, painful, excruciating feeling of anguish brought about by the realisation of the loss of someone integral to all you are as an individual. I was, therefore, not surprised to find that I suffered a strong reactive depression to my loss.

Sadness is another emotion that comes and goes. I feel sadness when I think what might have been, sadness at an event that seems so futile, sadness that I did not notice what was going wrong and I could not change events. I think this is true of bereavement in general, but perhaps it is heightened when death comes through suicide.

There is also the experience of emptiness. An empty chair, an empty place at the table, an empty seat in the car, and emptiness at your side when you go shopping or meet friends, an emptiness around the house, and so on. With a suicide death all those scenarios of emptiness bring back the events leading to the trauma of the loss. Perhaps along with other types of loss that involve a sudden death, the trauma of the event has gradually to wane before any of the emptiness can be filled with happy memories of the past. Even then I have found that remembering happy times is also painful because those times have gone. I trust that in the future, when adjustment to my new situation has become more familiar, I will find that happy memories will console me.

Frequently people told me that things would get better. How often had I said this to others in the past? But now I wanted to shout and say, " Maybe, but what about now? What about the pain at this point in time? How will I get through this day? What is there in the future?" I also found myself thinking that I never wanted to be responsible for anyone again, to love and care about someone deeply, because the pain of separation is just so awful. I also found myself wishing I could disappear. I would lie in bed wondering how people managed to disappear, dreaming up ways of just going off 'somewhere' never to return. Essentially I knew that this was a form of denial of all that had happened, but I was surprised at myself for thinking in this way.

The loss of an individual who is very dear and central to our life is a trauma whatever the circumstances. So often the view is expressed that one type of loss is worse than another, yet in discussion with the bereaved the sense of loss of someone very close seems to me to be equally devastating across a variety of circumstances. How then do we measure whether one experience of bereavement is greater than another? I do not think we can measure our losses in those terms, but we can highlight problems specific to the type of bereavement we have experienced and as such to the particulars of a death by suicide.

First of all with suicide there is the moral problem. Morality is an area of life which categorises ways of behaving into right and wrong, codes that lie at the heart of our criminal justice system and govern society. The act of suicide appears as a self-chosen death and is thus regarded as wrong. Suicide seems to go against the very laws of nature and our philosophical model of existence, where the belief is held that the desire and fight for survival lies at the core of our existence. However, adhering to the moral principle of right and wrong, and the philosophical principal of the instinct for survival, assumes a rational and healthy mind. It is my belief that the mind of the person who is driven to suicide is neither rational nor healthy, even though hours before they might have appeared so. I have thought that in some ways suicide is the result of a 'brain attack' one minute the person is in control, the next minute control is lost. I compare it to a person who is fit and healthy, running and full of life one minute, then suddenly drops dead. In a split second of time a change takes place in the person's biological functioning, a difference which changes life into death. People do not seem to have any difficulty in accepting that the heart, for example, can be beating and working normally one second, then the next second stops. However, it seems that there is a problem in accepting the fact that the reasoning part of the brain can be functioning one moment, then due to chemical or biological changes, reasoning and reality are lost and this can lead to suicide.

During the time since Tonie's death I have spoken to people who in the past have been driven to attempting suicide. The message that comes across each time is the experience of loss of control. One person explained, "It is like being on a roller coaster that is hurtling out of control, you are totally unable to stop the power within you driving you towards self destruction. No matter how much you are loved, how deep your faith, none of that influences you at this stage. When I look back I cannot relive that dreadful feeling, but I have no doubt whatsoever about its existence and its power to blot out reason." For those of us bereaved by suicide, we have to wrestle with these moral and philosophical problems linked to suicide and reconcile them for ourselves against the backdrop of our own experience, beliefs and ideologies.

I have come to the conclusion that Tonie was severely depressed and the depression obliterated her sense of self-preservation. She was in an irrational state of mind unable to judge the true right/wrong of her situation. She was compelled to suicide because, within her, an urge existed over which she had no control; she did not choose suicide she was driven to suicide. I believe it is likely that, in thousands of cases of suicide, the person has had no choice. Their death is a result of being at the extreme end of the scale of the debilitating and serious condition of depression. I know this belief does not account for every form of suicide but given that about 70% of suicides are believed to be linked with depression[12] it is relevant to many of us who have been bereaved in this way. In addition, recent brain implants carried out on people suffering chronic depression are showing very promising results, with one patient describing the effect as 'a black cloud lifting, the room lightening, increased spontaneity.' The fact that implants reducing excessive activity in the 'cingulate gyrus 25' area of the brain confirm for me that suicidal depression has a strong physical element affecting reasoning and perception of reality.

Unfortunately, because of the moral issues around suicide we get caught up in the criminal justice system, another particular aspect of suicide bereavement. The death has to be investigated to ensure there are no suspicious circumstances. The police, who search for clues to discover what has happened to the person we love, invade our privacy. In my case I was extremely lucky to have a police officer who dealt with Tonie's suicide with care and sensitivity, but that is not always the case, and caustic or flippant remarks can be deeply hurtful, as well as the lack of communication about what is happening.

Particular to our kind of bereavement is the nature of the inquest, where we may feel we are being judged, we have to give a testimony and be questioned - in contrast say to an inquest relating to the death of someone close to us killed by a stranger in a road traffic accident. Going to court, no matter how informal, still carries that feeling of a place where judgments take place. The inquest hangs over us as we wait for a date and time to appear in court. I knew the inquest was about bringing Tonie's death to a conclusion, but I still felt as though I was being judged, even though that was not so.

Furthermore a suicide death often involves 'evidence' in the form of notes, as in Tonie's case. Shortly after her death I decided to destroy the copies I had made of Tonie's note to me, and other notes the police had found in her room, obviously written in the days leading up to her complete breakdown. I knew that no matter how many times I read what she had written I would not be able to discover her thoughts and feelings in those final hours. I kept no newspaper cuttings or anything negative relating to her death. I made up my mind that I would concentrate on all the positive aspects of her life and our life together. I also tried to focus on the fact that her death had come early, as it does for many, rather than on the way she died. Instead of allowing guilt and a sense of responsibility to fill my mind I remembered the advice given to me by someone who said, "You were there to help Tonie bear her burden which you did for twenty-two years, but you were not able, or expected, to take it from her" and another person said, "You have done the work you were meant to do with Tonie and now you are called to move on."

The inquest procedure also means we can get caught in the backlash of social responses to our bereavement by the unthinking attitudes and comments made through ignorance among the people around us and by sensationalised media reporting. It is through the media and social responses from some sections of society that we realise that even though we are in the twenty-first century there still lingers a stigma, horror and condemnation towards suicide. There is a prevailing belief among many that depression is a choice that it is possible to 'snap out' of the condition. Sensational headlines and insensitive reporting often increases our pain; the survivors are rarely mentioned and little account is taken of the traumatising effect of a suicide death on those left behind.

Any death brings changes to our life that most of us resist. I recall many years ago during a retreat weekend I was conducting for the bereaved, when one of the participants spoke about the sudden loss of her husband and said, "No time is the right time for the death and loss of someone you love." How true this is, and when death comes through suicide, our hearts and minds resist such a tragic ending. Nevertheless, if we do not come to terms with our particular experience of suicide, and frame it within our belief system and life experience, then such a disaster takes not only the life of the person we have lost, but also destroys the quality of life of those left behind. It is not unknown for those bereaved by suicide to follow the same path, and I can understand this.

The effects of shock, both physically and psychologically, can be numerous and are not always recognised. For me, as I have mentioned, the signs were overt. I screamed so loudly that my neighbours in a detached property across from me could hear me! My counsellor said it was possible that those outbursts of screaming that came unbidden, may well have prevented me suffering a mental breakdown. I had re-active depression and aches and pains in my muscles. I tackled these two particular difficulties by accepting anti-depressants from my doctor to help my system cope with the shock and gradually recover its own ability to control my moods and emotions. The anti-depressants also helped me to be able to talk through the things that worried me, because with them I had a measure of energy both mentally and physically. Without them I was withdrawn, lifeless, and lacking any motivation. I paid for regular clinical massage, which freed my muscles from tension and pain, and provided another outlet for the effect of shock on my whole being. There were times when I would go for the massage and it would release all the pent up emotions. I was fortunate that Lynn has a particular interest in the effects of shock and stress on the muscular and skeletal system and the application of massage to help this condition, so I was able to benefit from her skill and thus reduce the impact on my body of the physical manifestations of shock.

I found it a strain going to the Registrar's office to collect the death certificates. I needed several originals, which meant that it took longer than normal for them to be completed. I recall looking at the words FOUND DEAD IN FIELD and feeling nauseous. Peter had offered to come with me, and we sat there in silence neither of us wanting to talk. The Registrar tried to strike up a conversation about the nature of Tonie's death, but Peter and I could only answer with the briefest of replies, we didn't want to talk. When we came out of the office I cried and said to Peter, "Will it never end?" I meant all the formalities you have to deal with in the event of any death; they seem to go on forever.

All of us who are bereaved have to deal with changes to billing addresses, banks, wills and the like. When death has been through suicide it is difficult to speak with a complete stranger on those occasions where you are called to discuss the nature of the death. I burst into tears on several occasions when I had to talk about Tonie's death. I was however, met with kindness and patience, which eased the problem, but nevertheless I found it embarrassing and at times distressing.

Getting through first anniversaries and special occasions can be tortuous. Unlike most people I did not find Christmas time particularly difficult because Tonie and I had always kept Christmas low key. What have been difficult are birthdays and the summer months, because these were the times we made special. I was shocked at just how much I dreaded my birthday, but my friends were aware of this and they helped me through. I was also fortunate that Kate offered to go for a week's holiday with me in the first year after Tonie's death. We went on a holiday totally different from anything Tonie and I had done, and I found this helped a great deal.

In the midst of this grieving there have been rituals which have helped the process along. One ritual was going with Jean and Ian to plant wildflower seeds and bulbs along the edge of the path close to the ditch where Tonie died. My heart and spirit were lifted when I returned in the spring to see the heads of the daffodils dancing in the breeze as well as providing an unexpected blaze of colour. The other ritual was choosing a memorial stone and placing it at the crematorium. The crematorium gardens are so beautiful, peaceful and comforting even in the winter months. I planted cyclamen, fuchsias, bulbs and winter pansies around her memorial. I receive continued comfort and pleasure from going to the crematorium and looking after that little area of God's earth dedicated to her memory. When I am there I find comfort from seeing other people visiting and caring for their memorials and I feel I am doing something for Tonie, showing an expression of my continued love for her. Inevitably, crematoriums and graveyards cause us to ponder on the meaning of life and death, of religious belief and commitment. This is another aspect of my bereavement that I want to discuss in the next chapter, as it formed a large part of my thinking at the time of Tonie's death.

All is not lost

One of the first things I wanted to know about suicide was the current teaching on the subject, from the perspective of the Roman Catholic Church. Taking down the New Catechism[13] from the shelf, I found the relevant sections. Here I read that each individual life is sacred, given by God as a gift to be lived, not to be deliberately destroyed; the principle that self destruction is directly opposed to the normal yearnings of the human spirit to protect, preserve and promote life, to love oneself and to love others. With this I could only agree, but I wanted to know the Church's response to the person who, through suicide, appears to go against these aspirations. I found three guiding principles to help me. The Church teaches that: 'grave psychological disturbances, anguish or grave fear of hardship, suffering or torture can diminish the responsibility ...'[14] also 'we should not despair of the eternal salvation of persons who have taken their own lives. By ways known to Him alone God can provide the opportunity for salutary repentance. The Church prays for persons who have taken their own lives'[15]

The Church also refers to imputability in relation to suicide 'imputability and responsibility for an action can be diminished or even nullified by ignorance ...'[16]

Reading these words I found that I had not only been embraced by a caring and understanding local church, but also embraced into the fullness of the heart of the Church.

The Church, along with the State, both of which in the past condemned not only the person who suffered suicide, but those left behind, has now moved into the twenty-first century. Scientific, psychological and medical research have been able to influence religious thought and the law, moving thought away from interpreting suicide as a rational act of self-harm. Now the victim of suicide is no longer condemned by the church as an individual who has committed mortal sin subject to eternal damnation, or condemned by the law as a criminal. In times past those left behind suffered shame, a loss of personal integrity and dignity within their social circle, as well as loss of property and income, the latter being claimed by the state in previous centuries. Nevertheless, within society at large, I believe there lingers this medieval religious and social thinking. Even though a high percentage of the population here in the UK, for example, has no allegiance to or regard for Christian religious practice, many adhere to those archaic religious ways of thinking about suicide. I hope that as this century progresses these lingering beliefs will be completely replaced by enlightenment. We need this new understanding of suicide to pervade society encouraging a growing openness to discuss the subject and its consequences. I have been fortunate that for the most part I have experienced an enlightened response to my bereavement, but I know there are others who have not been as fortunate.

Friends, family, acquaintances and colleagues have shared their thoughts with me about Tonie's suicide and their religious beliefs. Here are some of the things people said:

'For me Tonie carried the cross with Jesus during those seven miles she walked in mental and physical pain. She was walking with Jesus not walking away from him and he was with her all the time.'

'I think God blessed Tonie by allowing her to walk out of this life into the next. She sort of walked and walked then lay down close to the earth and nature that she loved. In one way she passed naturally across the threshold of death into life beyond death, even though the circumstances are un-natural from our point of view.'

'I believe Tonie just wanted a release from her mental and physical pain and God answered her prayer even though we do not understand it.'

Tonie left a note telling me she had prayed and prayed and pleaded with God asking him, "Where are you?" At the time of her death I screamed and shouted at God. "Why didn't you answer her prayer, Why? Why? Why? Why did she have to suffer like this? Why didn't you help me to perceive her suffering and her pain? Where are you in all this mess?" There were no replies to the many questions, only tears, and exhaustion of mind and body. Then came a letter through the post from my sister-in law containing the following thoughts:

How do we understand?
Your friend, my friend our friend ...
... one day woke up
Her body in pain and her future uncertain
The Lord knew how much she was suffering and
Said he had a new role for her
He reached down and lifted
Her spirit to Heaven
Tonie is now sat with the Lord
He needed an Angel
Your angel, my angel, our angel
Yes we can understand
We do understand

Belief in angels is a characteristic of Catholicism. Belief in angels has been present since creation and their existence has been proclaimed in Christian scripture as well as in other belief systems throughout history. In their nature angels are spiritual beings linked to Christ, who is the source of the angelic world. They are his servants who carry out his work; they are as thousands of mirrors reflecting the immeasurable power and love of God for his creation, reaching out into the universe linking heaven and earth. The church teaches that, 'as purely spiritual creatures angels have intelligence and will, they are personal and immortal creatures.'[17] Tonie's death has reminded me of, and renewed my faith in, this angelic world. The reminder of angels came not only through the words of my sister-in-law but also in other ways.

Since Tonie's death Lynn has not only helped remove the physical effects of shock from my muscles through massage, but also by bringing her personal spirituality to those sessions, part of which is her belief in the angelic world. There have been a number of occasions when she has expressed a sense of Tonie's presence during my massage. Two incidents in particular strengthened my faith in the angelic presence. Lynn had met Tonie only once some considerable time before her death. Someone had advised Tonie to try massage as a relief for her muscle pain. Tonie made one visit to Lynn and while she benefited from the massage she did not think that it would bring the lasting benefit she was looking for. This visit was two years prior to her death so Lynn did not get to know Tonie. Yet, at the end of one session of massage Lynn said she could feel Tonie's presence at her left side and could hear Tonie laughing. Tonie laughed a great deal, it was a strong character trait, but Lynn knew nothing of that side of her character. On another occasion Lynn went very quiet during the massage session. Afterward she asked me, "Did Tonie ever wear white?" "Yes," I replied. "Years ago, when we first started out, we wore white dresses and green headscarves, white as a symbol of joy and hope, and green as a symbol of new life in Christ. We did not retain this style but still kept the colours of green and white in our dress for formal/religious occasions." Lynn had seen and felt the presence of Tonie wearing a white dress and stood at the right side of the couch as she gave me my massage. On both these occasions I was not aware of Tonie's presence, there was no eerie or artificial atmosphere, neither was Lynn engaged in any effort to 'get in touch' with Tonie, it was just a natural presence that came unbidden, a gift from God to strengthen and guide me.

Some months after Tonie's death a close friend told me that she had experienced a very strong sense of Tonie and a fleeting image of her at a flower festival. This friend was stood near a large flower arrangement that was representative of the resurrection. The friend was not thinking about Tonie, she was just going about her role as a host for the flower festival. She explained, "I turned to look at that flower arrangement as I found it particularly beautiful and I saw a woman bending down in front of it. I was aghast. I thought that is Tonie! Then someone tapped me on the shoulder to ask me a question and when I turned back she was gone. I feel certain she was present at that moment and the fact that she was at the resurrection flower arrangement confirmed for me that she is with God."

Another strong reminder of Christ working through the angelic presence was in Neill, who led the search for Tonie and cared for me throughout that dreadful time. I recall thinking on several occasions he was like a guardian angel, guiding and protecting me. In addition, others who came into contact with him, both men and women, commented to me that they thought that there was something 'special' about him. No one ever defined what he or she meant by 'special'. I would say it was a type of aura around him, of which I guess he was not at all conscious. I had been thinking about this when I saw a book entitled *The Angelic Year*.[18] It was in a sale, so I bought it. It is beautifully illustrated and I was uplifted as I dipped into its pages. I found myself pondering on the fact that I had perceived Neill as an 'angel' while he was responsible for the search for Tonie. I began looking for male figures within the angelic realm. I found St. Michael the Archangel, whose feast is in September, the month Tonie went missing. Among the attributes accorded St. Michael the Archangel are that he is the guardian of the soul, particularly at the moment of death. He is the defender of justice, and defender of all who wish to know God's mercy. He is believed to rule over, among others, the Catholic Church and the Police. I believe that the presence of God through his Archangel Michael was with Neill at the time of Tonie's disappearance and death. Neill guarded, defended and helped me; he stood at my side when I was weak and vulnerable.

Some months after Tonie's death I noticed an advert for a walking pilgrimage during Holy Week known as Student Cross.[19] Being in my fifties I wondered whether I would be able to walk with this group of people. On making enquiries, I was told that there were some mature people in the group and that I would be welcome. So, on the Friday prior to Good Friday, I found myself in a church hall in Kettering with twenty-eight other people, most of whom were strangers, preparing for the 120-mile walk to Walsingham.

That week of walking helped me in many ways. The physical demand of walking fifteen miles or so a day, following a large wooden cross being carried in relays by three members of the group at a time, provided a focus and a goal each day. It also helped break the cycle of endless questions, and continually reliving the events of Tonie's death, again and again. Living rough for a week, bedding down in a sleeping bag in a church hall each night with only basic facilities, meant attention had to be given to the physical demands of the pilgrimage. The undemanding companionship of my fellow walkers was invaluable. There was no pressure to talk about my particular pain of that time. I could just walk along with my own thoughts and be engaged in the general chatter.

During the course of the day, the group would stop to rest from carrying the cross, to eat, to chat and to have a short meditation known as a 'station'. A station involves a member of the group talking about some aspect of their Christian life and journey that they have been thinking about during the course of walking to Walsingham. My pain was still raw so I was unable to contribute to this part of the pilgrimage. All I could do was to keep walking or talk about day-to-day things like how many more miles there were to walk, and what we would be cooking for supper and so on. But, a week after the pilgrimage, I chose to write to my fellow walkers to share with them some of the thoughts and experiences I had been unable to talk about during the week. What follows is an extract from that letter to my fellow pilgrims …

…Remembering and reconciliation was one of the themes during our journey. As I walked along, many memories crowded in on me of the days Tonie and I had spent crossing the Fen to go to Norfolk to have a few days peace and quiet together … As I walked along, I reached out to God to ask Him to reconcile my will to His and to help me not only accept Tonie's death, but to embrace it, even though I know I will never be able to understand. This reminded me that the acceptance of 'mystery' in our life is an essential part of our Christian commitment.

A great deal of my time was spent thinking and praying about Judas during our pilgrimage because of the fact that he was a victim of suicide. His name cropped up many times over the week and for the most part he presented among our group as a 'fly in the ointment', someone who made us feel uncomfortable and whose actions were unexplainable. But to my joy one of the people who offered us hospitality on our pilgrimage and shared our station spoke with great compassion towards Judas and for that I thank her. Here now are my reflections about Judas:

When Jesus said that one of his apostles would betray him it would appear from the Gospels that none of them knew that it was Judas. The apostles were shocked to think that one of them might be a traitor. Judas was part of the close community around Jesus and the fact that they did not suspect him suggests that he was loved and accepted by the group. Jesus also washed Judas's feet as he did the rest of the disciples. In the gospels other than that of St. John, Jesus is reported as saying that it would have been better had Judas not lived. Was that because Jesus knew the tremendous suffering Judas had delivered upon himself, and that he was aware of the anguish and despair Judas would experience? I believe that Jesus spoke those words with compassion and love towards Judas. In John's gospel Jesus says, 'One of you will betray me' and then gave Judas a piece of bread that had been dipped in the dish. This action of offering the bread to another was symbolic, in Jewish tradition, of a deep friendship. It gives us a clue that the pain of betrayal experienced by Jesus was likely to have been deep, because he loved Judas as much as the other disciples. When Judas left the table Jesus is not recorded in this gospel as having condemned him to the disciples who remained with him.

Did Judas betray Jesus any more or less than Peter who denied Jesus, or the apostles who ran away and left Jesus? We do not hear of any of them speaking up for and defending Jesus. The apostles had been with Jesus day after day experiencing His love for them, His faith in them, but they were doubters and they betrayed Jesus as much as Judas. However, they were able to live with their failure, they still had hope in the future. Perhaps for Judas the light of hope had gone from his life, and like the people we have loved and lost, he could not shake off the urge to self-destruct, that power overtook all reason.

I feel that I have shared in something of the betrayal Jesus felt when Judas let him down. Initially, I felt deeply hurt and betrayed by Tonie. Did she not know how much I loved her? Why couldn't she share her sense of despair with me? Why didn't she say she felt depressed or that she was thinking irrationally and feeling the urge towards self-destruction? I couldn't believe that she had hidden her thoughts from me because we had always been open and truthful with each other. How could she just walk out of my life? Was my love not good enough? I felt I had failed her completely and all that we had gone through together and achieved over the years had been a complete waste of time. What about our consecrated life how did that stack up against suicide? Much of who I am today is because of the great love, loyalty, trust and sharing we had had together over twenty-two years. I felt rejected when she had gone, but at the same time I felt an overwhelming compassion and love for her as I knew she must have been suffering a great deal to be driven to such a desperate measure.

Returning to Judas, I think most people might say of him that he was a betrayer, some might even go as far as to say that he would be condemned to hell for his actions. Why judge him on that final act of his life? Does it negate all that he did before? Let us think a little further; let us not judge him solely on this sad ending to his life. Judas was someone's son, his parents and extended family are likely to have been shocked and shamed by his death and grieved for his loss. His friends and the apostles would be hurt and bewildered by his action, and would be asking themselves if they could have helped him, or were they in some way responsible for what had happened. Judas had a history before the act recorded in the gospel. If we believe that Jesus is God, then God himself chose Judas to be one of his followers and there is much more to Judas than the gospel records – that is a thought which I think is worth dwelling upon.

What about the belief that those who take their own lives are damned to hell? I have never held that belief but have always been guided by the philosophy found in the book 'The Cloud of Unknowing'.[20] Here the unknown author guides us to judge an action but not to judge the person. Judgement is in God's hands. Tonie believed that for many people their 'hell' was experienced on earth. She had had an extremely traumatic childhood and she had to carry that hell of memories throughout her life and this coloured her belief in 'hell on earth.'

I do not believe that Tonie is in hell, whether you believe in hell as a place or a state of being. If at my own death I find I am wrong, then I know without doubt that I will have to go to hell too, because for me there could be no heaven if Tonie were not there. The God I believe I know and love would not separate Tonie from His love, or from me, because love of God and love of neighbour are inextricably bound together. If Tonie is not in heaven, then I have been deceived in my belief and experience of a god of infinite love and compassion. I read recently a reflection on the death of Jesus that said:

'there is no depth of human experience that Jesus cannot identify with or touch with his companionship ... nearly all forms of depression and meaninglessness involve no moral fault of the sufferer ... (author unknown)

It is often said that people who commit suicide have lost their faith, have turned their back on God. Tonie left notes, which showed that this assumption is not a universal fact. In her anguish she wrote, "God where are you?" Can we not hear Christ's words, "My God, My God, why have you forsaken me?" She also wrote, "Please, please God help me?" Tonie in her distressed and disturbed state of mind believed she was not lovable, that she was not fit to act as a mentor to people who sought her advice and that she was becoming a burden to me. At the time of her death she was not thinking rationally and therefore I believe we, who have not walked that desolate path toward self-annihilation, cannot judge her actions, we should show only compassion.

On the front of the booklet that Frank prepared for our pilgrimage there was the title;

'Reflections of those carrying the cross of the voiceless, forgotten and oppressed'

I felt as though I was carrying the cross with all those who lose someone to death by suicide. There are, according to the World Health Organisation, around one thousand suicides a week worldwide and around one hundred a week in Britain. For the greater part, these people are voiceless, they are unable to express their emotional and physical pain in words, it is expressed in their choice of death; they are often forgotten because suicide is still a social stigma. Those of us who are left behind do not like to say that the person we love died as a result of suicide. There is a sense that we are in some way responsible and that the hearer will be uncomfortable and perhaps horrified by such information. People who take their lives are oppressed in spirit and for many of us who are left behind we are oppressed by their death ...

Since writing that letter more than twelve months ago I continue my journey towards God silently carrying the heartache of Tonie's loss and suicide. I find the greatest consolation in the love and concern of my friends, family and the Church. They have not condemned Tonie, but shown compassion, they continue to remember her, to love her and in that I am consoled. At the same time they empathise with my continuing pain and understand that as a victim of suicide you do not just 'get over it' in a few months. I find strength in my personal prayer and the continuing prayer of the Church. It is these things which get me through the difficult days. They assist me to move very slowly away from the oppression, deep sadness and loss resulting from suicide towards acceptance of its mystery, a willingness to bear the pain and allow it to become a bearable part of myself. In addition to this I think back to a series of events that occurred around the time of Tonie's disappearance, death and cremation, which for some might be considered as coincidences. *The Oxford English Dictionary defines coincidences as 'a remarkable concurrence of events or circumstances without apparent causal connection'.* However, for me the events were linked so strongly with Tonie that I accepted them not as coincidences but as an affirmation from God that Tonie was safe, and as signs to comfort me in my distress.

As I mentioned earlier, Tonie and I had a joke between us concerning kingfishers, and I recounted how my brother and Ian had seen the kingfisher along the canal when searching for Tonie when she was missing. I have walked the canal frequently in recent years and never seen a kingfisher. I believed that the kingfisher was an affirmation that Tonie had walked along the canal and gradually it came to light that, on the afternoon that she went missing, she had been sighted on the towpath walking (as we now know) in the same direction as the kingfisher's flight.

Four days after Tonie had been found, Kate came to collect me to go for a walk and do some bird watching. We went to a local country park and I expressed my hope to see a bullfinch, as they are known to be at this location. We walked along and eventually came to the river. At this point the river is very wide and fast flowing. There were a number of birds on the water and Kate was explaining about mixed flocking and how you should always look closely, as it is likely that there will be more than one species of bird within the flock. Then out of the corner of my eye I noticed, to my left, the dark shape of a bird flying low and fast over the water. I drew Kate's attention and asked, "What is that bird Kate?" As she turned to look, it had reached a landing spot on the piers of a lock, across the river from us. "I think it is a Kingfisher. That is not common along this type of very wide open river environment." I could not locate the bird with my binoculars but Kate, who is far more experienced, did so and exclaimed, "Yes, it is a kingfisher and it is directly in front of us, sat on a ledge!" I found it with my binoculars and in that moment prayed, "Dear God, if Tonie is alright please let the kingfisher fly towards me." Then I said, "No, I should not ask for a sign I should believe." At that moment the kingfisher flew directly towards us and landed on the riverbank to the right of our feet. Kate and I stood and looked at the kingfisher and each other. Tears were pouring down my cheeks. The kingfisher stayed where it had perched until we moved then it flew off down the river. I told Kate of my silent prayer and her comment was that kingfishers are seen occasionally in this type of location but they are more likely to frequent smaller narrower rivers with overhanging branches. "Neither is it usual," she said, "for a kingfisher to fly directly towards human beings who are stood prominently on the bank of a river looking through binoculars. For the most part kingfishers fly away from you!"

Over a year later, I was walking with a friend along the River Lune. I had not seen this friend for many years. As we walked by the river she picked up a feather and said, "Look, this feather is shaped like an angel. I feel Tonie is here with us." I smiled and agreed, then turned towards the river and there was a kingfisher flying close to the water, the sunlight on its iridescent blue back. I had not spoken to this person about the significance for me of the angels or the kingfisher.

The other sign, for me, was the presence of larks. Around our home, larks are generally present each year during the breeding months. I recounted earlier that on the day Neill took me to the spot where Tonie had died, Kate noted that there were larks rising from the field and singing. Shortly after this I was preparing Tonie's memorial service and I came

103

across a poem which she had chosen at the time of her final vows. I decided to put into the memorial service booklet because of the content of the last two lines:

... He has come

Into his garden

Is it beautiful at last?

Are there flowers and perfumes?

I do not know

The garden is not mine but His

God asked only for

My little space

To be prepared

And given

This is

'garden'

for

Him

And my joy is full

Somewhere ....

There is the sound of water springing

And a lark is singing[21]

On the other side of the path, opposite the ditch where Tonie lay dying, is a pond. Whether it is formed from a natural spring or is manmade I do not know, but what is important to me is that, where God took Tonie to himself, there is water springing and larks singing.

During the time Tonie was missing, my nephew had a very vivid dream. He was sitting somewhere on stone or concrete. From this point, he could see a hill covered in trees. The hill was bounded by a fence and had a large pointed structure that appeared to come out of the top of the hill. He also dreamt that Tonie was in some way in a direct line to our home. A few hundred yards away from the ditch, where Tonie's body was recovered, is a wooded hill, bounded by a fence. There is not a tall pointed structure at the top of it, but close by are electric pylons. Plotting the grid references, on the ordnance survey map, of where Tonie's body was found and the location of our house, the same latitudinal line can be drawn between the two points. If you walk the seven miles along that latitudinal line from the side of our house where we have a stone patio you come to the field where Tonie died.

As I recounted earlier, I awoke one morning determined to walk the path Tonie had taken from our home to the ditch. There was another event on that day which I have not mentioned. As I turned onto the canal towpath, two larks ascended into the sky singing their hearts out. I stopped and looked at them. In that moment, they reminded me of how

Tonie and I had been in our life together. Two people retaining their individuality with space between them like these two birds, yet at the same time singing the same song, full of joy and hope, looking to the future together. I walked on. It took me three hours or more to arrive at the field and the ditch. I stood at the far end of the field unable to walk further as planting had taken place. I looked through the binoculars at the rubber glove overhanging the ditch. As I stood there, a single lark rose up above the ditch singing and rising into the air, free and full of joy. At the beginning of this walk there were two larks and here at the end only one, just as Tonie and I had been two, now one is taken and one left.

Any death inevitably causes us to question the existence of life after death, and the conclusions we come to will be formed by our life experience. There are those who hold the opinion that there is certainly no life after death, others that there is life after death but only for the select few, and the rest of us have a diversity of beliefs between those two poles. A good friend asked me, "Did Tonie's death make you think about life after death, about the belief in heaven, and what heaven is?" I replied, "Yes, but I had visited those questions many times before because of my interest in bereavement and care for those who are bereaved".

I have chosen to believe in life after death. I find inspiration and truth in the life and teachings of Christ and the Catholic Church, but I also think that if my faith proves unfounded and there is nothing after death I will not be disappointed because there will be no 'knowing or awareness'. Living with faith in Christ and believing in life after death makes my life here on earth richer and more meaningful. I was very interested to read in the Dalai Lama's *Little Book of Wisdom*[22] the following words relating to death and the Buddhist tradition ...

'In my daily practise of prayer I visualise eight different deities and eight different deaths. Perhaps when death comes all my preparations will fail. I hope not! I think these practices are mentally very helpful in dealing with death. Even if there is no next life there is some benefit if they relieve fear ...' This is testimony that even the most eminent spiritual leaders look doubt in the face, but choose to elect faith.

For me, heaven will be a new way of being in God, beyond my ability to comprehend in this life. It will be a moving into the wider universe; it will be a fuller and deeper unity with all those I love and the experience of love; it will be freedom from the hurts of earthly life and an awareness of realities as yet hidden. Mysteries will be unfolded, not least the mystery of those things most painful to us here on earth, which we are unable to understand. I envision life after death as an active process, although how this will manifest itself, obviously, I do not know. I think it might be by being in tune with the resonance of all nature, that I will become attuned to greater resonances out in the universe, opening me up to realities that are impossible to reach while we are embodied in our flesh. Thus a new awareness and way of being will emerge.

When Christ re-appeared to his apostles after the resurrection, they did not recognise him. Christ was changed in some radical way. He revealed Himself to his friends by certain words or actions that he had performed during his earthly life, and it was through these signs that they recognised Him. Christ had to link the past to the present in order for recognition to occur. We do not learn from the gospels why the apostles could not recognise Christ but in some way earth and heaven came together in those fleeting moments of contact after the resurrection.

Scientific research is continually discovering new realties and powers in our universe that show us there is still so much energy and power in and around us waiting to be discovered. Kathleen Fisher, a theologian and psychotherapist, perceives scientific development and life beyond death coming together when she writes in her thought-provoking book *Imaging Life After Death*[23] '... the worldview of quantum physics, which describes reality as an interconnected web of relationships, gives us new grounds for our experience of remembering and relating to those who have died, and for envisioning the social dimension of the resurrected body'. Alfred Tomatis a French Specialist in Ear, Nose and Throat conditions, a psychologist and educator wrote in detail in his autobiography of his experience while being in a state described by doctors as 'neuro-vegetative collapse'. The experience led him to make these bold statements 'we never die ... death does not exist ... beyond death I feel I shall not be lost.' [24]

Likewise, Teilhard de Chardin priest, scientist and mystic communicates, through his poetic and philosophical writing, in *Hymn of the Universe* his belief that life here on earth is part of our journey into the infinity of the mystery and love of God present throughout the Universe ... 'If we are to be assimilated into him [God] he must first break down the molecules of our being so as to recast and remould us ... death puts us into that state which is organically necessary if the divine fire is to descend upon us ... What was of its nature void, empty, a regression into plurality, can now in every human being become plenitude and unity in God ...' [25]

After effects, from operations for organ transplants, suggest that organs of the body have 'memories and abilities' that are passed on to recipients from the donor organ. [26] For example, someone may receive a heart transplant from a talented musician and the donor, who previously had no such talent or ability, suddenly acquires musical ability. There are savants who see numbers as colours and designs and can perform the most complicated mathematical computations; these rare people see the world around them in the form of numbers! Rupert Sheldrake an eminent biologist in his book *A Sense Of Being Stared At* [27] explores methods to measure or quantify what he calls the 'sixth sense'. He makes it clear that he does not consider this sense to be 'a spiritual sense' but rather a biological function of telepathic awareness. As a biologist, he is attempting to reveal powers and resonances within our biological existence that make people aware of each other even when they are not together. There are members of the neuroscience community who are looking at ways to measure spiritual experiences and verify their nature. Some of their work and findings are recorded in the book *Destructive Emotions* [28] Perhaps these are the early steps towards a stronger bond between the scientific community and the spiritual community out of which the presence of God in our Universe will be understood and life after death understood as more than a glorified version of our present existence. Nevertheless, by the very nature of the expanse of creation, and all that it entails, it would seem to me that the element of mystery has to remain for God to be God who is forever to be discovered. And because God is ever to be discovered, so too is redemption possible beyond death. God offers his love through all time and beyond time. Those who appear to have rejected God completely will have the opportunity to choose God beyond this life. Beyond death will be a new reality and all people will remain within reach of God, no one is damned forever, there will be an eternal opportunity to choose God. I view life after death in this way because creation and our life on earth is in a constant state of change, so why should eternity be static?

It has been my experience, that to come to terms with death as a result of suicide, it is necessary to accept that you are not responsible for, or the cause of, the person following this path, no matter what the circumstances. Not even if the person who has died tried to put the blame upon you. The individual driven to suicide is in an abnormal state of mind over which you can have no control.

In the early days of my bereavement, my nephew wrote these words to me, 'through time you will realise that you cannot judge yourself on what has happened. I am sure at this present time you are still asking yourself a lot of questions with only dark black spaces to fill the answers you seek …I am certain that if you could have helped Tonie with her condition you would have done so. But ask yourself what could you have done? Unfortunately words and love alone could not have changed the situation … Tonie must have known this, that there was nothing you could have done. This is why she did not trouble you with the burden she carried; to trouble you with her worries would have only amplified the problem for herself. I am so sure of it. Do not forget her life span had already been chosen before you met her …'

I was comforted by his words in those early days of grief. Time has brought me to the realisation that I am not responsible for her death. I hope that those of you who read this book will find your way to freedom, so that you too can be free of carrying a sense of responsibility and guilt for the loss and death you experienced. Instead may you find comfort in recalling the positive experiences of your life with the person you so dearly loved.

I have found it helpful to understand the grieving process, to work through unresolved issues with friends and a professional counsellor, to face the reality of the situation, and to seek help for the physical problems that arose due to shock and finally to formulate positive plans for the future. I believe that to rebuild my future I had to reconcile the many doubts, fears and feelings that followed Tonie's death. There is a future out there for all of us bereaved by suicide, which can be enriching and fulfilling, but we have to reach out to it.

I have let others help me and I have not allowed myself to feel ashamed of Tonie's death but see it for what it is, a crippling and distressing illness. We who have been bereaved by suicide are the ones who can help change the ways of thinking about suicide and support research into this complex illness, which not only took away the person special to us, but also has resulted in terrible pain for us and our families and friends. May you find your way through the situation and consequences that have arisen as a result of being bereaved by suicide. Your story, your questions, your life experience and how you resolve your bereavement will be different. But resolve it you must, to live again.

Now, at the very beginning of the third millennium let us look forward with hope that more help for suicidal illness will come about, as well as increased compassion and understanding towards the victim and growing support and guidance for those of us so bereaved.

APPENDIX

Random thoughts

The following poem was written at a time when I had been dwelling on the fact that across all cultures there is still a great deal of medieval thought and belief within our societies surrounding the tragedy, mystery and horror of suicide. I felt that as we are now in the 21st century it was time that these thoughts and beliefs be challenged in the light of our social, religious, and psychological development of the past five hundred years.

Suicide in the 21st Century

Now, now is the time to stride on
No longer shamed by ancient muse
Damning those held in suicide's throes

Now, now is the time to sing a new song
Let comfort and kindness, be our news
Rescuing, healing, suicide's woes

Eighteen weeks after Tonie went missing I took up teaching once more, not in my own business but working free-lance with adults. My first student was a young woman who, at our point of meeting, was in her early twenties. As we got to know each other, it transpired that she had already experienced four significant deaths in her life. This dyslexic student had a strong interest in poetry. We used poetry as the starting point for extending her literacy skills and building her confidence to get back into study and work. The book she chose at that time was the 'BBC The Nation's Favourite Poems of Remembrance' 2003

Over the weeks of working together, we selected a number of poems to read and discuss. Among the selection of poems was Christine Rossetti's poem 'Remember'. We considered what we thought the people we had loved and lost would say to us on the subject of remembering. This is what I thought Tonie would say.

Remembering

Remember not my pain and despair
Nor wonder what dark thoughts led me there
These dwellings will not bring you peace
Rest in faith – our loving God has given me ease

Recall instead our love and laughter
Our years of happiness is what matters
Be sure that I remain always by your side
And there will stay until death brings you to me on the tide

Our God will forever us unite
Embraced in love and filled with light
Friends and foes reconciled as one
Lifted beyond the sorrows of earthly days now run.

Approximately a year after Tonie's death I was teaching a few dyslexic students who were preparing for GCSE English. We had been discussing the use of alliteration as a poetic device. I was writing a phrase to illustrate the point - found in the first line of the poem - the rest followed spontaneously. What I found strange about this poem is that I had no intention of writing it; neither was I aware of Poe's famous poem 'The Raven' and its theme of death. It was some time later whilst pondering on the significance of the Raven, that I realised I had some vague recollection of a myth that when the Ravens leave the Tower of London it will be the death of the monarchy in Britain and that the Raven in mythology is linked with death and doom. The fact that this image arose spontaneously seems to link with those theories relating to how in our sub-conscious we carry within us a 'collective consciousness' and an imprint of our evolution, and that all of us are linked with each other by some forces and influences greater than ourselves.

Suicide

Crammed deep down in the darkness
Crouches the hidden one
No one knows its name
So they call it Raven

It has no wings
Yet it flies
It has no voice
Yet it speaks with power

Always lurking
Travelling, weaving through the
Recesses of the mind
Searching, longing through the years

Now, now it comes,
The Raven for its prey
No warning
Only death gives witness to its visitation

Separation

One taken, one left, how well we know the pain
A life so precious, a spirit so kind
A much loved face now lost
We know the pain

How harsh the cold mountain air
How shadowed the valleys we walk
These barren landscapes of our soul
We know the pain

Tears trickle, then flood like torrents
Down steep mountain sides
Memories ebb and flow as mists in our mind
We know the pain

We have stood on mountain tops
Inhaled the beauty of their vistas
Shared the rich river valleys
But not today, today we only have our pain

And what of tomorrow? Will the pain ever leave?
Some say yes, others say no
We have no answer - only our pain
And it seems to us an endless refrain

The tides and seasons ebb and flow
The sun and moon come and go
Minds, hearts and bodies meet and part in life's continuous song
This, this song of life will bear us through our pain
And in it, one day I know, we shall our love regain.

This poem was written shortly after a neighbour of mine had lost his wife, and about twelve months after Tonie's death. I had been thinking about Jennie's husband and the sense of separation that death brings, an experience only too familiar to me.

Useful Books relating to Suicide Bereavement

Alvarez Al **The Savage God A study of Suicide** (2002) Bloomsbury

Cox David/Carrington Candy **Aftershock** (2003) Broadman Holman Tennessee

Dykstra Robert **She Never said Goodbye** (1989) Harold Shaw Illinois

Fine Carla **No Time To Say Goodbye** (1997) Broadway America with reprint in UK Doubleday

Helen Maggie **Coping with Suicide** (2002) Sheldon Press

Jamison Key Redfield **Night Falls Fast** (2000) Vintage Books

Murray Parkes Colin **Bereavement Studies in Grief in Adult Life** (1996) Penguin

Robinson Rita **Survivors of Suicide** (2001) Career Press USA

Smolin Ann/Guinan John **Healing after the suicide of a loved one** (1993) Simon & Schuster New York

Wertheimer Alison **The Special Scar** (2001) Brunner and Routledge

******

National Helpline – Survivors of Bereavement by Suicide (S.O.B.S.)

Tel: 0870 2413337 9a.m. – 9 p.m. every day

End Notes

---

[1] http//www.rcpsych.ac.uk/press/preleases
[2] http/www.Samaritans.org/know/suicidestats.uk
[3] Dykstra Robert (1989) *She Never Said Goodbye* Pub. Harold Shaw
[4] Wertheimer Alison (2000) *The Special Scar* Pub. Brunner & Routledge
[5] Macintyre Anne 1998 *M.E.* (1998) Pub. Thorsons
[6] Marty Haugen CD 'All are Welcome' GIA Publications Inc*
[7] Schlegel Hymns Old & New No. 59 (1983) Pub.Kevin Mayhew
[8] David Harkins 1959 www.poeticexpressions.co.uk
[9] Kubler Ross Elisabeth *On Death and Dying* (1997) Pub.Simon & Schuster Inc
[10] Styron William *Darkness Visible* p58 Pub.Jonathan Cape Ltd. 1991
[11] Kay Redfield Jamison *Night Falls Fast* (2000) Pub.Vintage Books
[12] The Times June 28 2005 Brain Implants for Depression
[13] Catechism of the Catholic Church (1994) Pub.Geoffrey Chapman
[14] Ibid
[15] Ibid
[16] Ibid
[17] Ibid P76-77
[18] Wauters Ambika *The Angelic Year* (2000) Pub. Carroll Brown
[19] www.studentcross.org.uk
[20] *Cloud of Unknowing and Other Works* Pub. Penguin Classics (1961)
[21] Anon – Carmel Quidenham Norfolk
[22] The Dalai Lama's *Little Book of Wisdom* (2002) Pub.Carroll Brown
[23] Fischer Kathleen *Imaging Life After Death* (2005) Pub. SPCK
[24] Tomatis Alfred (1991) *The Conscious Ear* p.191-197 Pub. Station Hill Press
[25] Teilhard de Chardin *Hymn of the Universe* (1965) p.130 Pub. Collins
[26] www.nexusmagazine.com/article/Cellularmemories
[27] Sheldrake Rupert *A Sense of Being Stared At* (2004) Pub. Arrow Books
[28] Daniel Goleman/The Dalai Lama *Destructive Emotions* (2003) Pub. Bloomsbury